Crochet Patterns
GNOMES
Christmas Edition #2

Traditional Christmas Gnomes 7

Fireworks 13

Gingerbread Gnome 17

Gingerbread Cookies 39

Christmas Chef 31

Christmas Guard 47

Poinsettia 23

Baby Angel 74

Christmas Bells 53

Snowmen 85

Candy Gnome 57

Angel 63

Christmas Elf 97

Lady Angel 69

Gnome Lumiere 79

Christmas Tree 105

Christmas Cup 91

Recommendations

YARN

Blend: cotton and acrylic fiber yarn
Yarn Weight: Sport/Fine
Yarn length/weight: approx. 160 meters (174 yds) per 50 gram ball.
Yarn ideas: YarnArt Jeans (used for designs from this book), Scheepjes Softfun, Sirdar Snuggly Replay DK.
If you plan on using a yarn different from the recommended one, make sure to select a crochet hook suitable for your chosen yarn. It is important to achieve a tight gauge/tension to prevent the toy stuffing from showing through the crocheted fabric. You may need to use a smaller hook size than what is recommended on the yarn label.

TOOLS

Recommended Hook in Metric Size Range: 2.5 mm
Note: We will be using a smaller hook size than what is recommended on the yarn label. This is to achieve a tight fabric that prevents stuffing from showing up.
Stitch markers.

TIPS BEFORE YOU START

Single Crochet "V" and "X"
The typical method to make a single crochet is to insert your hook into a stitch, yarn over, pull through, yarn over, pull through both loops. This method makes a 'V' stitch.
The other lesser-known method to make a single crochet is to insert your hook into a stitch, yarn under, pull through, yarn over, pull through both loops. This method makes an 'X' stitch. Please, note that I use SC "x".

Scan to watch a video tutorial

LIFEHACK

You can use this crocheted item as a door stop.
Make a small fabric bag (a size 10cm x 15cm or so) (as well you can use a finished small pouch bag and stitch along an opening when a bag is filled with some filler).
Fill with Pebbles, cat litter, washed sand, rice or beans (food may attract insects).
When you have done a first round with decrease at a bottom of each gnome you can put the bag inside along with the rest of the filler and continue crocheting closing the bottom.

GAUGE/TENSION

Rd 1	6SC in magic ring, tighten the ring [6]. Mark beg of rd in each rd.
Rd 2	INC in each st around [12]
Rd 3	*(SC in next st, INC in next st)from*rep x6 [18]
Rd 4	*(SC in next st, INC in next st, SC in next st) from*rep x6 [24]
Rd 5	*(SC in next 3sts, INC in next st)from*rep x6 [30]
Rd 6	*(SC in next 2sts, INC in next st, SC in next 2sts) from*rep x6 [36]

Size: Ø 4.5-5cm
If you are going to use different from the required yarn, you need to grab a crochet hook that is suitable for your yarn, and the gauge/tension should be tight enough, so the toy stuffing doesn't show up through the crocheted fabric

TIPS

How to use QR codes: Download a QR code scanning app on your smartphone or use the integrated feature in some phones' camera. Align the QR code in the app's viewfinder, ensuring it is well-lit and in focus. The app will automatically scan the QR code. Wait for a few seconds. After scanning, click on the website URL associated with the QR code. Your smartphone's browser will open the link for you to explore further.

Abbreviations (US terms)

St(s)	Stitch/es	
Rd	Round	
Ch	Chain stitch	

Scan to watch video tutorials

SC	Single Crochet "X"
DC	Double Crochet: yarn over, insert hook in stitch, yarn over, pull through stitch, [yarn over, pull through two loops] twice
sl st	Slip Stitch: insert hook in stitch, yarn over, pull through both loops on hook
hdc	Half Double Crochet: yarn over, insert hook in stitch, yarn over, pull through stitch, yarn over, pull through all 3 loops on hook
hdc-whb	Half double crochet worked in horizontal bar (third loop)
SC2tog	Single crochet two together: Insert hook into stitch and draw up a loop. Insert hook into next stitch and draw up a loop. Yarn over, draw through all 3 loops on hook.
prev	previous
INC	Increase: single crochet in one stitch twice
Ch-space	Chain-space
BLO/FLO	Back loop only/ Front Loop only
WS/RS	Wrong side/ Right side

*(...) from *rep x	work instructions within parentheses as many times as directed by x
Surface slip stitch	Place a thread behind the fabric, insert hook into the crocheted fabric from the front to the back and grab yarn on hook, pull a loop through to the front. Insert hook from front to back and pull a loop to the front side and through the loop on the front of the fabric to create a surface slipped stitch.
BPsc	Back post single crochet. Back Post - Insert hook from back to front between the posts of the first and second stitches, and then from front to back again between the posts of the second and third stitches.

How to change a color

Before you work the final yarn over on the last stitch of a row\round in the old color, drop old yarn and then pick up the new one with your hook. Pull through a loop of the new yarn to finish the old stitch. The working loop will be in the new color. Continue, keeping the old yarn at the wrong side or cut it off depending on the pattern. Pic 1

Tapestry crochet

Change the color as it's described in the section "How to change a color". Then carry your non- working yarn inside of the stitches (a blue thread in pic 2).

Traditional Christmas Gnomes

SIZE: 30 cm/ 11.8 in

COLORS AND YARN			TOTAL FOR 1 GNOME
Red		Yarn Art Jeans 90	Approx. 25g/80meters
Pearl grey		Yarn Art Jeans 49	Approx. 15g/50meters
Wheat		Yarn Art Jeans 05	Approx. 5g/15meters
White		Yarn Art Jeans 62	Approx. 7g/20 meters
Bright Yellow		Yarn Art Jeans 35	A little amount
Black		Yarn Art Jeans 53	Approx. 3g/10meters

TOOLS:
Crochet Hook 2.5 mm; Tapestry needle

OTHER MATERIALS:
Stuffing approx. 50 g (for 1 gnome)

CROCHET STITCHES:
St(s),Ch, hdc, SC, INC, DC, sl st, SC2tog

To effectively mark the beginning of each round, it is recommended to use a contrasting thread. This thread should be kept in place until your work is completed.

HAT
(WORK IN CONTINUOUS ROUNDS)

Rd 1	**Red:** 6SC in magic ring [6] tighten the ring. Mark beg of rd in each rd.
Rd 2	*(INC in next st, SC in next st)from*rep x3 [9]
Rd 3-12	SC in each st around [9]
Rd 13	*(SC in next st, INC in next st, SC in next st) from*rep x3 [12]
Rd 14	SC in each st around [12]
Rd 15	*(SC in next 3sts, INC in next st)from*rep x3 [15]
Rd 16	SC in each st around [15]
Rd 17	*(SC in next 2sts, INC in next st, SC in next 2sts) from*rep x3 [18]
Rd 18	SC in each st around [18]
Rd 19	*(SC in next 5sts, INC in next st)from*rep x3 [21]
Rd 20	SC in each st around [21]
Rd 21	*(SC in next 3sts, INC in next st, SC in next 3sts) from*rep x3 [24]
Rd 22	SC in each st around [24]
Rd 23	*(SC in next 7sts, INC in next st)from*rep x3 [27]
Rd 24	SC in each st around [27]
Rd 25	*(SC in next 4sts, INC in next st, SC in next 4sts) from*rep x3 [30]
Rd 26	SC in each st around [30]
Rd 27	*(SC in next 9sts, INC in next st)from*rep x3 [33]
Rd 28	SC in each st around [33]
Rd 29	*(SC in next 5sts, INC in next st, SC in next 5sts) from*rep x3 [36]

Rd 30	SC in each st around [36]
Rd 31	*(SC in next 11sts, INC in next st)from*rep x3 [39]
Rd 32	SC in each st around [39]
Rd 33	*(SC in next 6sts, INC in next st, SC in next 6sts) from*rep x3 [42]
Rd 34	SC in each st around [42]
Rd 35	*(SC in next 13sts, INC in next st)from*rep x3 [45]
Rd 36	SC in each st around [45]
Rd 37	*(SC in next 7sts, INC in next st, SC in next 7sts) from*rep x3 [48]
Rd 38	SC in each st around [48]
Rd 39	*(SC in next 15sts, INC in next st)from*rep x3 [51]
Rd 40	SC in each st around [51]
Rd 41	*(SC in next 8sts, INC in next st, SC in next 8sts) from*rep x3 [54]
Rd 42	*(SC in next 26sts, INC in next st)from*rep x2 [56] Change to Black in last st.
Rd 43-45	**Black:** SC in each st around [56] Change to Red in last st of Rd 45. Cut off Black
Rd 46	**Red:** SC in each st around [45]

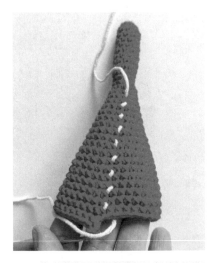

CONTINUE - HAT BRIM
(WORK IN CONTINUOUS ROUNDS)

Rd 47	Ch2, *(DC FLO in next 6sts, 2DC FLO in next st) from*rep x3, hdc FLO in next st, SC FLO in next 5sts, INC FLO in next st, SC FLO in next 5sts, hdc FLO in next st, *(2DC FLO in next st, DC FLO in next 6sts) from*rep x3, DC FLO in next st, sl st in 2nd Ch [64] Note: the body will be crocheted into stitches BLO of Rd 46 later

Rd 48	Ch2, (the first DC work in the same stitch as sl st) DC in next 25sts, hdc in next st, SC in next 12sts, hdc in next st, DC in next 24sts, sl st in 2nd Ch [64]
Rd 49	Ch2, (the first DC work in the same stitch as sl st) *(DC in next 7sts, 2DC in next st)from*rep x3, hdc in next st, SC in next 6sts, INC in next st, SC in next 6sts, hdc in next st, *(2DC in next st, DC in next 7sts) from*rep x3, DC in next st, sl st in 2nd Ch [72]
Rd 50	SC in next 72sts around [72], sl st in 1st st of rd

Cut off Red and weave in

BODY
(WORK IN CONTINUOUS ROUNDS)

Rd 1	Hold the hat upside down, with **Pearl grey** work BLO into stitches of Rd 46: SC BLO in each st around [56]
Rd 2	**For male gnome:** SC in next 11sts, SC BLO in next 5sts (an arm will be attached to theses sts), SC in next 8sts, SC BLO in next 8sts (a beard will be attached to theses sts), SC in next 8sts, SC BLO in next 5sts (an arm will be attached to theses sts), SC in next 11sts. **For female gnome:** SC in next 11sts, SC BLO in next 5sts (an arm will be attached to theses sts), SC in next 3sts, SC BLO in next 3sts (a braid will be attached to these sts), SC in next 3sts, SC BLO in next 6sts (a nose will be attached to these sts), SC in next 3sts, SC BLO in next 3sts (a braid will be attached to these sts), SC in next 3sts, SC BLO in next 5sts (an arm will be attached to theses sts), SC in next 11sts [56]

Rd 3-7	SC in each st around [56]
Rd 8	*(SC in next 13sts, INC in next st)from*rep x4 [60]
Rd 9-12	SC in each st around [60]
Rd 13	*(SC in next 7sts, INC in next st, SC in next 7sts) from*rep x4 [64]
Rd 14-15	SC in each st around [64]
Rd 16	*(SC in next 3sts, SC-2tog, SC in next 3sts) from*rep x8 [56]
Rd 17-18	SC in each st around [56]
Rd 19	*(SC in next 5sts, SC-2tog)from*rep x8 [48]
	Stuff. Stuff as you work
Rd 20-21	SC in each st around [48]
Rd 22	SC BLO in each st around [48]
Rd 23	*(SC in next 2sts, SC-2tog, SC in next 2sts) from*rep x8 [40]
Rd 24	*(SC in next 3sts, SC-2tog)from*rep x8 [32]
Rd 25	*(SC in next st, SC2tog, SC in next st)from*rep x8 [24] Stuff. Stuff as you work.
Rd 26	*(SC in next st, SC2tog) from*rep x8 [16]
Rd 27	SC2tog x8 [8]

Cut off a thread, leave a long tail for sewing. Using this tail and a tapestry needle pull the tail through the last stitches FLO and tighten the opening. Weave in

HAT BRIM DECORATION

Rd 1	Hold the hat upside down, with White work into stitches of Rd 49 of the HAT BRIM on the right side: *(Ch1, sl st in next st) from*rep around Cut off a thread and weave in

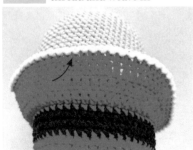

ARMS (make 2)
(WORK IN CONTINUOUS ROUNDS)
STEP 1 ARMS

Rd 1	**Wheat:** 5SC in magic ring [5] tighten the ring
Rd 2	INC in each st around [10]
Rd 3-5	SC in each st around [10] Change to Red in last st of Rd 5. Cut off Wheat
Rd 6-7	**Red:** SC in each st around [10]
Rd 8	SC BLO in each st around [10]
Rd 9-17	SC in each st around [10]

Cut off a thread leaving a long tail for attaching purposes

STEP 2 CUFF

Rd 1	**White:** work into stitches FLO of Rd 7: SC FLO in each st around [10]
Rd 2	SC in each st around [10]

Cut off a thread and weave in

Use NOSE pattern on page 110
Use BEARD pattern #1 on page 110
Use POMPON pattern on page 111

HAT DECORATION

Rd 1	**Bright Yellow:** Ch23, sl st in the first Ch to join in round
Rd 2	sl st in each st around [24]

Cut off a thread, leave a long tail for attaching purposes

BRAIDS (make 2)
White:

Section #1	Chain 25, SC in 2nd st from hook, SC in next 23 sts [24]
Section #2	Chain 25, SC in 2nd st from hook, SC in next 23 sts [24]
Section #3	Chain 25, SC in 2nd st from hook, SC in next 23 sts [24]

Cut off thread leaving a long tail for attaching purposes

BOOTS (make 2)
(WORK IN CONTINUOUS ROUNDS)

Rd 1	**Red:** 6SC in magic ring [6] tighten the ring
Rd 2	INC in each st around [12]
Rd 3	*(SC in next st, INC in next st) from*rep x6 [18]
Rd 4-5	SC in each st around [18]
Rd 6	*(SC in next st, SC2tog)from*rep x6 [12]
	Stuff. Stitch edges together by SC in next 6 stitches inserting your hook through both layers and closing the opening.

Cut off a thread leaving a long tail for attaching purposes

ASSEMBLING

For the male gnome: sew the nose on the beard(pic 1), and then sew the beard on the body under the hat brim in front to 8 stitches FLO of Rd 1.

For the female gnome, sew the nose to 6 stitches FLO of Rd 1 of the body under the hat brim. Pic.2.

Pic.3-4 For the female gnome: sew the braids on the body under the hat brim in front to 4 stitches FLO of Rd 1 on both sides. Sew the nose to 6 stitches in front of the body. Sew the boots on the body to stitches FLO of Rd 21 on both sides.

Pic. 5 Attach the buckle on the black part of the hat above the nose.

Pic. 6 Sew the arms on the body under the hat brim to 5 stitches FLO of Rd 1 on both sides.

Pic. 7 Hold the body upside down and sew the boots on the body to stitches FLO of Rd 21 on both sides.

Sew or glue the pompom on the hat.

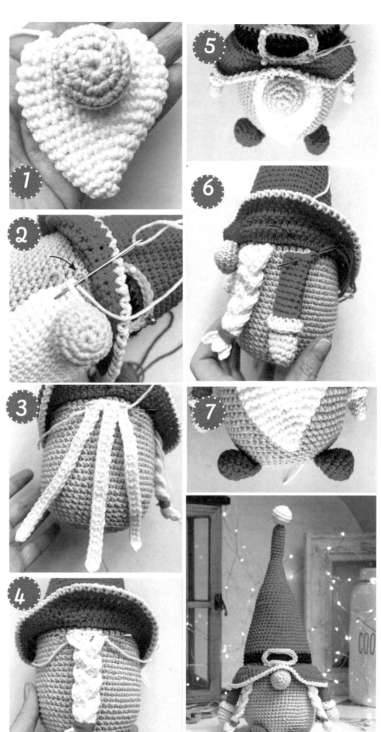

Fireworks

SIZE:
23 cm/
9 in

COLORS AND YARN

TOTAL FOR A PROJECT

Color		Yarn	Total
Red	★	Yarn Art Jeans 90	Approx. 20g/64meters
White	☆	Yarn Art Jeans 62	Approx. 15g/48meters
Wheat	★	Yarn Art Jeans 05	Approx. 7g/25meters
Bright Yellow	★	Yarn Art Jeans 35	Approx. 10g/32meters
Turquoise	★	Yarn Art Jeans 81	A little amount
Dark Green	★	Yarn Art Jeans 82	A little amount

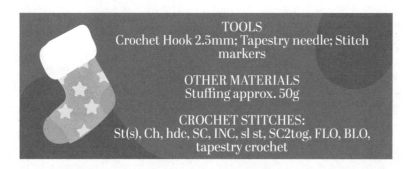

TOOLS
Crochet Hook 2.5mm; Tapestry needle; Stitch markers

OTHER MATERIALS
Stuffing approx. 50g

CROCHET STITCHES:
St(s), Ch, hdc, SC, INC, sl st, SC2tog, FLO, BLO, tapestry crochet

To effectively mark the beginning of each round, it is recommended to use a contrasting thread. This thread should be kept in place until your work is completed.

STEP 1. HAT
(WORK IN CONTINUOUS ROUNDS)

Rd 1	**Red:** 6SC in magic ring [6] tighten the ring
Rd 2	*(SC in next st, INC in next st)from*rep x3 [9]
Rd 3	SC in each st around [9]
Rd 4	*(SC in next st, INC in next st, SC in next st)from*rep x3 [12]
Rd 5	*(SC in next st, INC in next st, SC in next st)from*rep **x4** [16]
Rd 6	SC in each st around [16]
Rd 7	*(SC in next 3sts, INC in next st)from*rep x4 [20]
Rd 8	SC in each st around [20]
Rd 9	*(SC in next 2sts, INC in next st, SC in next 2sts) from*rep x4 [24]
Rd 10	SC in each st around [24]
Rd 11	*(SC in next 5sts, INC in next st)from*rep x4 [28]
Rd 12	SC in each st around [28]
Rd 13	*(SC in next 3sts, INC in next st, SC in next 3sts) from*rep x4 [32]
Rd 14	SC in each st around [32]
Rd 15	*(SC in next 7sts, INC in next st)from*rep x4 [36]
Rd 16	SC in each st around [36]
Rd 17	*(SC in next 5sts, INC in next st) from*rep **x6** [42]
Rd 18-19	SC in each st around [42] Change to White in last st of Rd 19. Place a stitch marker into the last st for later.

we are going to work a tapestry crochet technique when a no-working color is carried inside of the stitches. When it's time to change to a new color do it in last stitch of a working color (see page 5),

Rd 20	*(White: SC BLO in next 3sts, **Bright Yellow:** SC BLO in next 3sts)from*rep around [42] Then, SC in next st and mark be of rd - we replaced the beg of rd and will do that in each round where it's stated.
Rd 21-30	*(White: SC in next 3sts, **Bright Yellow:** SC in next 3sts)from*rep around [42] SC in next st
Rd 31	*(White: SC in next 3sts, **Bright Yellow:** SC in next 3sts)from*rep around [42] Change to White in last st. Cut off Bright yellow
Rd 32	**White:** *(SC FLO in next 3sts, INC FLO in next st, SC FLO in next 3sts)from*rep x6 [48]
Rd 33	SC in each st around [48]
Rd 34	*(SC in next 7sts, INC in next st)from*rep x6 [54]
Rd 35	SC in each st around [54]
Rd 36	*(SC in next 4sts, INC in next st, SC in next 4sts)from*rep x4 [60]
Rd 37	sl st in each st around [60]

Cut off a thread and weave in

Step 2

STEP 2. BORDER ON THE HAT

Rd 1	Hold the hat upside down and join **Red** to the st with a stitch marker and work: (SC FLO in next 3sts, INC FLO in next st, SC FLO in next 3sts) from*rep x6 [48]
Rd 2	SC in each st around [48]
Rd 3	sl st in each st around [48]

Cut off a thread and weave in

STEP 3. BODY

| Rd 1 | Hold the hat upside down and with **Red** work BLO into stitches of Rd 31 of step 1: SC BLO in each st around [42] |

Rd 2	SC in next 9sts, SC BLO in next 4sts(an arm will be attached to theses sts), SC in next 4sts, SC BLO in next 8sts (a nose will be attached to these sts), SC in next 4sts, SC BLO in next 4sts(an arm will be attached to theses sts), SC in next 9sts [42]
Rd 3-5	SC in each st around [42]
Rd 6	*(SC in next 3sts, INC in next st, SC in next 3sts)from*rep x6 [48]

Rd 7-10	SC in each st around [48] Stuff. Stuff as you work
Rd 11	*(SC in next 5sts, INC in next st) from*rep **x8** [56]
Rd 12-13	SC in each st around [56] Place a stitch marker into the second stitch of Rd 13 to mark a point where we will start working the decoration on step 5
Rd 14	SC BLO in each st around [56]
Rd 15	SC in each st around [56]
Rd 16	*(SC in next 5sts, SC2tog) from*rep x8 [48] Stuff
Rd 17-18	SC in each st around [48]
Rd 19	SC BLO in each st around [48] Note: we will work a stand into these stitches FLO in step 4.
Rd 20	*(SC in next 2sts, SC2tog, SC in next 2sts)from*rep x8 [40]
Rd 21	*(SC in next 3sts, SC2tog) from*rep x8 [32]
Rd 22	*(SC in next st, SC2tog, SC in next st)from*rep x8 [24]

| Rd 23 | *(SC in next st, SC2tog) from*rep x8 [16] Stuff |
| Rd 24 | SC2tog x8 [8] |

Cut off a thread, leave a long tail for sewing. Using this tail and a tapestry needle sew pull the tail through the last stitches FLO and tighten the opening. Weave in

STEP 4. STAND

Hold the gnome upside down and with **Red** work into stitch FLO of Rd 18 of the body: Ch1, hdc FLO in each st around [48]
Cut off a thread and weave in

STEP 5. TWO-COLORED BRAID

Use White and Dark green, the pattern and video tutorial - page 19 (Gingerbread Gnome). Work into stitches FLO of Rd 13. Start from the stitch marker.

Use Wheat and the nose pattern on page 110

Use Bright Yellow and the beard pattern #2 on page 110

ARMS (make 2)
(WORK IN CONTINUOUS ROUNDS)

Rd 1	**Wheat:** 5SC in magic ring [5] tighten the ring
Rd 2	INC in each st around [10]
Rd 3-5	SC in each st around [10] Change to Red in last st. Cut off Honey Caramel
Rd 6-17	**Red** SC in each st around [10]

Cut off a thread leaving a long tail for attaching purposes

STARS (MAKE 1 IN EACH COLOR)

Rd 1	**Turquoise/Bright Yellow:** 10SC in magic ring [10] tighten the ring
Rd 2	*(Ch3, sl st in 2nd st from hook, hdc in next ch, skip next st of Rd 1, sl st in next st of Rd1) from*rep x5

Cut off a thread leaving a long tail for attaching purposes

WICK

White: Chain 6. Cut off a thread.
Bright yellow: Make a tassel and attach it with the wick to the top.

ASSEMBLING

Sew the nose on the beard and then all together sew under the hat brim in front to 8 stitches FLO of Rd 1 of the body.
Sew the arms on the body under the hat brim in front to 4 stitches FLO of Rd 1 of the body on both sides.

Sew the stars on the hat

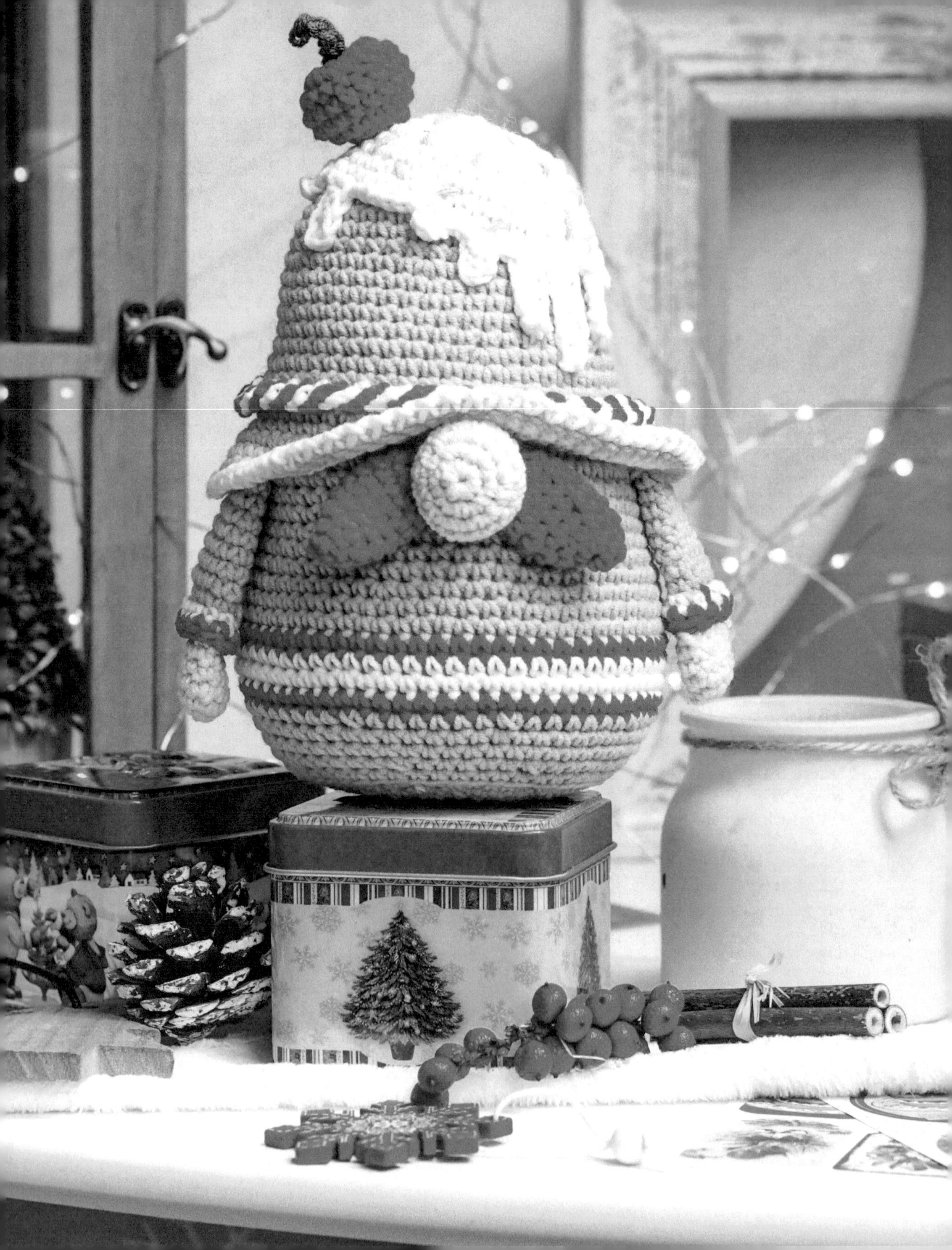

Gingerbread Gnome

SIZE: 17cm/ 6.7in

COLORS AND YARN			TOTAL FOR A PROJECT
Beige		Yarn Art Jeans 07	Approx. 30g/96meters
Red		Yarn Art Jeans 90	Approx. 10g/32meters
Wheat		Yarn Art Jeans 05	Approx. 5g/15meters
Off-White		Yarn Art Jeans 03	Approx. 10g/32 meters
Grass Green		Yarn Art Jeans 69	A little amount

TOOLS
Crochet Hook 2.5mm; Tapestry needle

OTHER MATERIALS
Stuffing approx. 40g

CROCHET STITCHES:
St(s), Ch, SC, hdc, INC, sl st, SC2tog, FLO, BLO

To effectively mark the beginning of each round, it is recommended to use a contrasting thread. This thread should be kept in place until your work is completed. When it comes to changing colors, remember to cut off the thread as specified in the pattern.

HAT
(WORK IN CONTINUOUS ROUNDS)

Rd 1	**Beige:** 6SC in magic ring [6] tighten the ring. Mark beg of rd in each rd.
Rd 2	INC in each st around [12]
Rd 3	*(INC in next st, SC in next st)from*rep x6 [18]
Rd 4	*(SC in next st, INC in next st, SC in next st) from*rep x6 [24]
Rd 5	*(SC in next 3sts, INC in next st)from*rep x6 [30]
Rd 6-7	SC in each st around [30]
Rd 8	*(SC in next 2sts, INC in next st, SC in next 2sts) from*rep x6 [36]
Rd 9-10	SC in each st around [36]
Rd 11	*(SC in next 5sts, INC in next st)from*rep x6 [42]
Rd 12-13	SC in each st around [42]
Rd 14	*(SC in next 3sts, INC in next st, SC in next 3sts) from*rep x6 [48]
Rd 15-17	SC in each st around [48]
Rd 18	*(SC in next 11sts, INC in next st) from*rep **x4** [52]
Rd 19-20	SC in each st around [52]
Rd 21	SC BLO in each st around [52] Place a stitch marker in the second stitch of this round to mark the starting point for crocheting the hat decoration.
Rd 22	*(SC in next 6sts, INC in next st, SC in next 6sts) from*rep x4 [56]

CONTINUE - HAT BRIM
(WORK IN CONTINUOUS ROUNDS)

Rd 23	SC FLO in each st around [56] **Note:** later, to create the body, we will be crocheting into these stitches BLO
Rd 25	*(SC in next 7sts, INC in next st) from*rep **x7** [63] Change to Off-White in last st. Leave Beige on WS
Rd 26	**Off White:** *(SC in next 4sts, INC in next st, SC in next 4sts)from*rep x7 [70] Change to Beige in last st. Leave Off-White on WS
Rd 27	**Beige:** SC in each st around [70] Change to Off-White in last st. Cut off Beige
Rd 28	**Off-White:** *(Ch1, sl st in next st)from*rep around

Cut off a thread and weave in

BODY
(WORK IN CONTINUOUS ROUNDS)

Rd 1	Hold the hat upside down, With **Beige** work BLO into stitches of Rd 22: SC BLO in each st around [56] . Mark beg of rd in each rd.
Rd 2	SC in next 11sts, SC BLO in next 5sts (the arm will be attached to these sts), SC in next 8sts, SC BLO in next 8sts (the beard will be attached to these sts), SC in next 8sts, SC BLO in next 5sts (the arm will be attached to these sts), SC in next 11sts [56]
Rd 3-8	SC in each st around [56]
Rd 9	*(SC in next 3sts, INC in next st. SC in next 3sts)from*rep x8 [64]
Rd 10-11	SC in each st around [64] Change to Red in last st. Leave Beige on WS
Rd 12	**Red:** SC in each st around [64] Change to Off-White in last st. Leave Red on WS
Rd 13-14	**Off-White** SC in each st around [64] Change to Red in last stitch. Cut off Off-White
Rd 15	**Red:** SC in each st around [64] Change to Beige in last stitch. Cut off Red
Rd 16	**Beige:** *(SC in next 3sts, SC2tog, SC in next 3sts) from*rep x8 [56]
Rd 17-18	SC in each st around [56]

Rd 19	*(SC in next 5sts, SC2tog) from*rep x8 [48]
	Stuff. Stuff as you work
Rd 20-21	SC in each st around [48]
Rd 22	SC BLO in each st around [48]
Rd 23	*(SC in next 2sts, SC2tog, SC in next 2sts)from*rep x8 [40]
Rd 24	*(SC in next 3sts, SC2tog) from*rep x8 [32]
Rd 25	*(SC in next st, SC2tog, SC in next st)from*rep x8 [24]

TWO-COLORED BRAID (FIND QR CODE WITH A VIDEO BELOW)

Hold the gnome upside down. Join **Off-White** to stitch FLO marked with the stitch marker in Rd 20 and work: Chain 3 (pic. 1), drop the Off-white loop off your hook. Join **Red** to the stitch located to the right of the stitch where we made 3ch from. Work Chain 3 (pic.2),

1) work SC into the next available front loop on the left (pic. 3),

2) Chain 3 (pic.4),

3) drop Red loop off your hook,

4) grab the Off-white loop back on your hook (pic.5),

5) (note: always keep your work in front of the dropped part, it will help to "twist colors") SC into the next available loop on the left (pic.6),

6) Chain 3,

7) drop the Off-white loop off your hook,

8) grab the Red loop

Repeat steps 1-8 around. Cut off a thread and weave in

Rd 26	*(SC in next st, SC2tog)from *rep x8 [16]
Rd 27	SC2tog x8 [8]

Cut off a thread, leave a long tail for sewing. Thread the tapestry needle with the tail and pull it through the FLO of the stitches on the last round and tighten. Weave in

Scan to watch a video tutorial "Two-colored braid #1"

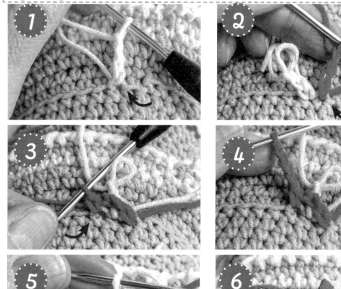

ARMS (make 2)
(WORK IN CONTINUOUS ROUNDS)

STEP 1. ARMS

Rd 1	**Wheat:** 5SC in magic ring [5] tighten the ring
Rd 2	INC in each st around [10]
Rd 3-5	SC in each st around [10]

Change to Beige in last st. Cut off Wheat

Rd 6-7	**Beige:** SC in each st around [10]
Rd 8	SC BLO in each st around [10]
Rd 9-16	SC in each st around [10]

Cut off a thread leaving a long tail for attaching purposes

STEP 2. CUFF

Rd 1	**Off White:** work into stitches FLO of Rd7: SC FLO in each st around [10]
Rd 2	**Red:** SC in each st around [10]

Cut off a thread. Weave in

CREAM ON THE HAT (WORK IN CONTINUOUS ROUNDS)

Rd 1	**Off White:** 7SC in magic ring [7] tighten the ring
Rd 2	INC in each st around [14]
Rd 3	*(INC in next st, SC in next st)from*rep x7 [21]
Rd 4	*(SC in next st, INC in next st, SC in next st) from*rep x7 [28]
Rd 5	*(SC in next 3sts, INC in next st)from*rep x7 [35]
Rd 6	*(SC in next 2sts, INC in next st, SC in next 2sts) from*rep x7 [42]
Rd 7-9	SC in each st around [42]

Continue: <u>make drips</u>:
SC in next 3sts,
1st drip: Chain 2, hdc in 2nd Ch from hook, hdc in stitch of the main part as Ch2, skip next st of the main part, SC in next st of the main part;
2nd drip: Chain 3, hdc in 2nd Ch from hook, hdc in next st of chain, hdc in stitch of main part as Ch3, skip next st of the main part,
SC in next 2sts of main part,
3rd drip: Chain 4, hdc in 2nd Ch from hook, hdc in each st of chain, hdc in stitch of the main part as Ch4, skip next st of the main part, SC in next st of the main part,
hdc in next st of the main part, 3hdc in next st of the main part, SC in next st of the main part;
4th drip Chain 2, hdc in 2nd Ch from hook, hdc in stitch of the main part as Ch2, skip next st of the main part, SC in next st of the main part,
5th drip Chain 3, hdc in 2nd Ch from hook, hdc in next st of chain, hdc in stitch of the main part as Ch3, skip next st of a main part, SC in next st of the main part,
6th drip Chain 4, hdc in 2nd Ch from hook, hdc in each st of chain, hdc in stitch of main part as Ch4, skip next st of the main part, SC in next st of the main part,
7th drip Chain 6, hdc in 2nd Ch from hook, hdc in each st of chain, hdc in stitch of main part as Ch6, skip next st of the main part, SC in next st of the main part,
8th drip Chain 5, hdc in 2nd Ch from hook, hdc in each st of chain, hdc in stitch of the main part as Ch5, skip next st of the main part, SC in next st of the main part,
9th drip Chain 2, hdc in 2nd Ch from hook, hdc in stitch of the main part as Ch2, skip next st of the main part, SC in next st of the main part,
hdc in next st of the main part, 3hdc in next st of the main part, hdc in next 3sts of the main part, SC in next 2sts of the main part.
REPEAT patterns for the **4th-7th drips**. When it's done, work SC to end of the round

Cut off a thread and weave in or leave a long tail for attaching purposes in case of sewing (you also can glue this part on the hat with a hot glue gun)

CHERRY
(WORK IN CONTINUOUS ROUNDS)

Rd 1	**Red:** 6SC in magic ring [6] tighten the ring
Rd 2	INC in each st around [12]
Rd 3	*(SC in next st, INC in next st)from*rep x6 [18]
Rd 4-5	SC in each st around [18]
Rd 6	*(SC in next st, SC2tog) from*rep x6 [12]

Cut off thread leaving a long tail for attaching purposes. Stuff the cherry with a small amount of stuffing

STICK

Grass Green: Ch6, Sl st in 2nd st from hook, sl st in next 4 sts

Cut off thread leaving a long tail for attaching purposes.

Use Wheat and the NOSE pattern on page 110.
Use Red and MUSTACHES pattern on page 110.

ASSEMBLING
Attach the cream part with drips on the hat, sew or glue.

Sew or glue the cherry on the hat.

Sew mustache on the body under the hat brim.

Attach the nose above the mustache

Sew the hands on the body under the hat brim

Poinsettia Gnome

Gnome is 24cm/ 9in

COLORS AND YARN

Color		Yarn	TOTAL FOR A PROJECT
Red		Yarn Art Jeans 90	Approx. 15g/48meters
Beige		Yarn Art Jeans 07	Approx. 25g/80meters
Wheat		Yarn Art Jeans 05	Approx. 5g/15meters
Brown		Yarn Art Jeans 40	Approx. 7g/20 meters
Bright Yellow		Yarn Art Jeans 35	A little amount
Grass Green		Yarn Art Jeans 69	Approx. 10g/32meters

TOOLS
Crochet Hook 2.5mm; Tapestry needles

OTHER MATERIALS
Stuffing approx. 40g

CROCHET STITCHES:
St(s), Ch, hdc, SC, INC, SC2tog, sl st

To effectively mark the beginning of each round, it is recommended to use a contrasting thread. This thread should be kept in place until your work is completed.

HAT
(WORK IN CONTINUOUS ROUNDS)

Rd 1	**Beige:** 6SC in magic ring [6] tighten the ring [6] Mark beg of rd in each rd
Rd 2	*(INC in next st, SC in next st)from*rep x3 [9]
Rd 3-5	SC in each st around[9]
Rd 6	*(SC in next st, INC in next st, SC in next st) from*rep x3 [12]
Rd 7-8	SC in each st around [12]
Rd 9	*(SC in next 3sts, INC in next st)from*rep x3 [15]
Rd 10-11	SC in each st around [15]
Rd 12	*(SC in next 2sts, INC in next st, SC in next 2sts) from*rep x3 [18]
Rd 13-14	SC in each st around [18]
Rd 15	*(SC in next 5sts, INC in next st)from*rep x3 [21]
Rd 16	SC in each st around [21]
Rd 17	*(SC in next 3sts, INC in next st, SC in next 3sts) from*rep x3 [24]
Rd 18	SC in each st around [24]
Rd 19	*(SC in next 7sts, INC in next st)from*rep x3 [27]
Rd 20	SC in each st around [27]
Rd 21	*(SC in next 4sts, INC in next st, SC in next 4sts) from*rep x3 [30]
Rd 22	SC in each st around [30]
Rd 23	*(SC in next 9sts, INC in next st)from*rep x3 [33]
Rd 24	SC in each st around [33]
Rd 25	*(SC in next 5sts, INC in next st, SC in next 5sts) from*rep x3 [36]

Rd 26	SC in each st around [36]
Rd 27	*(SC in next 11sts, INC in next st)from*rep x3 [39]
Rd 28	SC in each st around [39]
Rd 29	*(SC in next 6sts, INC in next st, SC in next 6sts)from*rep x3 [42]
Rd 30	SC in each st around [42]
Rd 31	*(SC in next 13sts, INC in next st)from*rep x3 [45]
Rd 32	SC in each st around [45]
Rd 33	*(SC in next 7sts, INC in next st, SC in next 7sts)from*rep x3 [48]
Rd 34	SC in each st around [48]

CONTINUE - HAT BRIM

Rd 35	*(SC FLO in next 15sts, INC FLO in next st)from*rep x3 [51]
Rd 36	*(SC in next 8sts, INC in next st, SC in next 8sts) from*rep x3 [54]
Rd 37	*(SC in next 4sts, INC in next st, SC in next 4sts) from*rep x6 [60]
Rd 38	*(SC in next 9sts, INC in next st)from*rep x6 [66]
Rd 39	*(SC in next 5sts, INC in next st, SC in next 5sts) from*rep x6 [72]
Rd 40	SC in each st around [72]
Rd 41	*(SC in next 11sts, INC in next st)from*rep x6 [80] Change to Red in last st. Cut off Beige

Rd 42	**Red:** sl st BLO in each st around [80]

Cut off Red and weave in

BODY
(WORK IN CONTINUOUS ROUNDS)

Rd 1	Hold the hat upside down and with **Beige** work into stitches BLO of Rd 34: SC BLO in each st around [48] Mark beg of rd in each rd

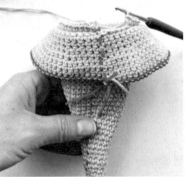

Rd 2	SC in next 20sts, SC BLO in next 8sts (we will attach a beard with nose to these sts), SC in next 20sts [48]
Rd 3	SC in next 10sts, SC BLO in next 4sts (we will attach the arm here), SC in next 20sts, SC BLO in next 4sts (we will attach the arm here), SC in next 10sts [48]

Rd 4-9	SC in each st around [48]
Rd 10	*(SC in next 5sts, INC in next st)from*rep x8 [56]
Rd 11-13	SC in each st around [56]
Rd 14	*(SC in next 3sts, INC in next st, SC in next 3sts) from*rep x8 [64]
Rd 15-16	SC in each st around [64] (place a stitch marker into 2nd st of Rd 16 to mark the spot where we will start crocheting a braid
Rd 17	SC BLO in each st around [64]
Rd 18	*(SC in next 3sts, SC2tog, SC in next 3sts)from*rep x8 [56]
Rd 19-20	SC in each st around [56]
Rd 21	*(SC in next 5sts, SC2tog) from*rep x8 [48]

Stuff. Stuff as you work.

Rd 22-23	SC in each st around [48]
Rd 24	SC BLO in each st around [48]
Rd 25	*(SC in next 2sts, SC2tog, SC in next 2sts)from*rep x8 [40]
Rd 26	*(SC in next 3sts, SC2tog) from*rep x8 [32]
Rd 27	*(SC in next st, SC2tog, SC in next st)from*rep x8 [24]

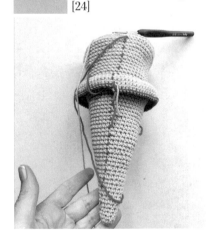

Rd 28	*(SC in next st, SC2tog) from*rep x8 [16]

Stuff

Rd 29	SC2tog x8 [8]

Cut off a thread, leave a long tail for sewing. Using this tail and a tapestry needle sew pull the tail through the last stitches flo and tighten the opening.

TWO-COLORED BRAID

Hold the gnome upside down.
Join **Red** to stitch FLO marked with the stitch marker (Rd 16) and work: Chain 4, drop the Red loop off your hook.
Join **Grass green** to the second stitch located to the right of the stitch where we made 3ch from. Work Chain 4,
1) work SC into the third available stitch st on the left,
2)Chain 4,
3)drop the Grass green loop off your hook,
4) get **Red** loop back on your hook,

5)(note: always keep your work in front of the dropped work, it will help to "twist colors") SC into the third stitch on the left,
6) Chain 3,
7) drop the Red loop off your hook,
8) get **Grass green** loop back on your hook,

Repeat steps 1-8 around.

Scan to watch a video tutorial "Two-colored braid #2"

STAND

Rd 1	Hold the body upside down and with **Beige** work into stitches FLO of Rd 23: Ch1, SC in next 48 sts, sl st in 1st st of rd to join the round [48]

Cut off a thread and weave in

ARMS (make 2)
(WORK IN CONTINUOUS ROUNDS)

STEP 1. ARM

Rd 1	**Wheat:** 5SC in magic ring [5] tighten the ring
Rd 2	INC in each st around[10]
Rd 3-5	SC in each st around [10]
	Change to Beige in last st. Cut off Wheat
Rd 6-7	**Beige:** SC in each st around [10]
Rd 8	SC BLO in each st around [10]
Rd 9-17	SC in each st around [10]

Cut off thread leaving a long tail for attaching purposes

STEP 2. CUFF

Rd 1	Hold the arm upside down and work into stitches FLO of Rd 7 with **Red**: sl st FLO in each st around [10]

Cut off a thread and weave in

RED BRACTS & LEAVES

(make 5x red, 5x grass green
(photo tutorial find on page 27)

Red/Grass Green: Chain 11

Rd 1	SC in 2nd st from hook, SC in next 8sts, 4SC in last stitch, work along the other side of the foundation chain: SC in next 8 sts, 4SC in next stitch [25]
Row 2	SC in next 8 sts [8] Turn
Row 3	sl st in 2nd st from hook, sl st in next st, Ch1, hdc in next 5sts, 2SC in next 3sts, SC in next 8sts [22], Turn
Row 4	sl st in 2nd st from hook, sl st in next st, Ch1, hdc in next 5sts, SC in next st, sl st in next st

Cut off a thread leaving a long tail for attaching purposes

FLOWER x1

Rd 1	**Bright Yellow:** 6SC in in magic ring[6] tighten the ring [6]
Rd 2	SC in each st around [6]

Cut off a thread, leave a long tail for sewing. Using this tail and a tapestry needle sew pull the tail through the last stitches FLO and tighten the opening.

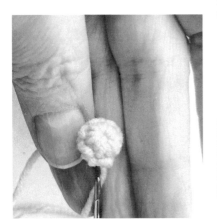

ASSEMBLING

1. Collect all the red bracts and thread them together, following the picture as a guide. Gather them tightly and secure them with multiple stitches.

2. Attach the flower in the middle by sewing or gluing it in place.

3. Fold the green leaves in a spiral pattern
4. Sew the flower onto the leaves to complete the arrangement.
5. Attach it to the hat by sewing or gluing

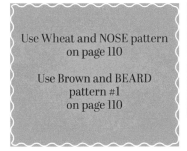

Use Wheat and NOSE pattern
on page 110

Use Brown and BEARD
pattern #1
on page 110

PHOTO TUTORIAL - BRACTS & LEAVES

Green\Red: Foundation chain:
Chain 11

SC in 2nd st from hook,

SC in next 8sts,

4SC in last stitch

work along the other side of the foundation chain: SC in next 8 sts,

ASSEMBLING

Sew the nose on the beard and then sew it on the body under the hat brim in front to 8 stitches FLO of Rd 1 of the body.

Sew the arms on the body under the hat brim in front to 4 stitches FLO of Rd 2 on both sides.

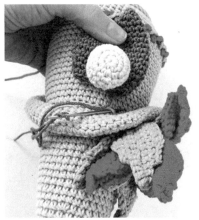

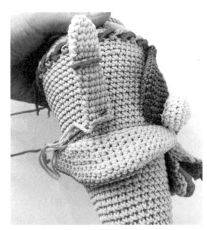

4SC in next stitch [25],

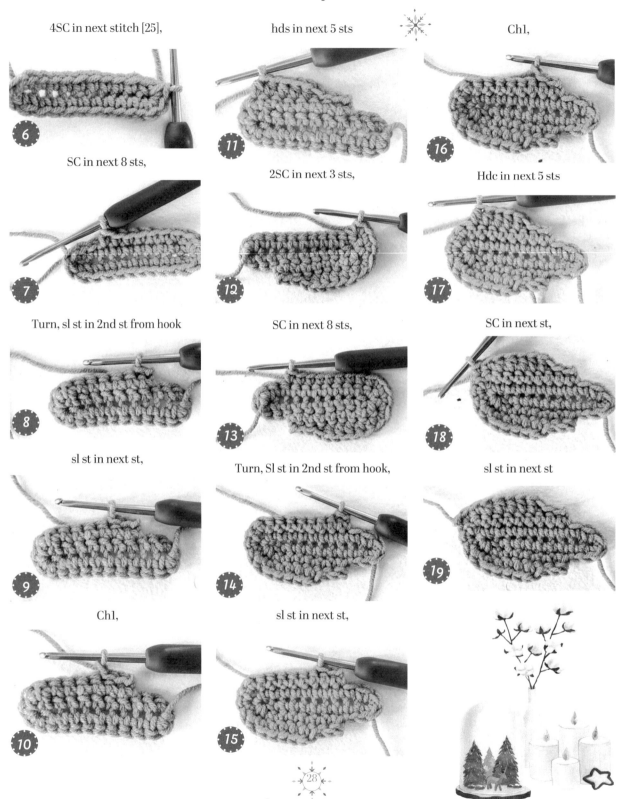

hds in next 5 sts

Ch1,

SC in next 8 sts,

2SC in next 3 sts,

Hdc in next 5 sts

Turn, sl st in 2nd st from hook

SC in next 8 sts,

SC in next st,

sl st in next st,

Turn, Sl st in 2nd st from hook,

sl st in next st

Ch1,

sl st in next st,

Christmas Chef

SIZE: 19cm/ 7.5in

COLORS AND YARN | TOTAL FOR A PROJECT

Color		Yarn	Total for a project
Wheat		Yarn Art Jeans 05	Approx. 7g/22meters
White		Yarn Art Jeans 62	Approx. 35g/112meters
Red		Yarn Art Jeans 90	Approx. 5g/16meters
Melange Black		Yarn Art Jeans 28	Approx. 5/16meters
Bright Green		Yarn Art Jeans 52	Approx. 10g/35meters
Dark Brown		Yarn Art Jeans 70	Approx. 7g/22meters
Light Grey (for ladle)		Yarn Art Jeans 46	Approx. 15/50meters

TOOLS
Crochet Hook 2.5mm; Tapestry needle

OTHER MATERIALS
Stuffing approx. 30g
Ø6-7mm x4 Red Bead (to imitate buttons)
Craft wooden stick (used to insert into a handle of a ladle)

CROCHET STITCHES: St(s), Ch, SC, INC, sl st, hdc, DC, SC2tog, FLO, BLO

To effectively mark the beginning of each round, it is recommended to use a contrasting thread. This thread should be kept in place until your work is completed.

STEP 1. Additional detail
(we will use it to separate a hat)
(work in continuous rounds)

Rd 1	**Wheat:** 6SC in magic ring [6] tighten the ring. Mark beg of rd in each rd
Rd 2	INC in each st around [12]
Rd 3	*(SC in next st, INC in next st) from*rep x6 [18]
Rd 4	*(SC in next st, INC in next st, SC in next st)from*rep x6 [24]
Rd 5	*(SC in next 3sts, INC in next st)from*rep x6 [30]
Rd 6	*(SC in next 2sts, INC in next st, SC in next 2sts)from*rep x6 [36]
Rd 7	*(SC in next 8sts, INC in next st)from*rep **x4** [40]

Cut off a thread and weave in

STEP 2. TORQUE
(work in continuous rounds)

Rd 1	**White:** 8SC in magic ring [8] tighten the ring
Rd 2	INC in each st around [16]
Rd 3	*(SC in next st, INC in next st)from*rep x8 [24]
Rd 4	*(SC in next st, INC in next st, SC in next st) from*rep x8 [32]
Rd 5	*(SC in next 3sts, INC in next st)from*rep x8 [40]

Rd 6	*(SC in next 2sts, INC in next st, SC in next 2sts) from*rep x8 [48]
Rd 7	*(SC in next 5sts, INC in next st)from*rep x8[56]
Rd 8	*(SC in next 3sts, INC in next st, SC in next 3sts) from*rep x8 [64]
Rd 9	*(SC in next 7sts, INC in next st)from*rep x8 [72]
Rd 10	*(SC in next 4sts, INC in next st, SC in next 4sts) from*rep x8 [80]
Rd 11	*(SC in next 9sts, INC in next st)from*rep x8 [88]
Rd 12	*(SC in next 5sts, INC in next st, SC in next 5sts) from*rep x8 [96]
Rd 13-20	SC in each st around [96]

Rd 21	*(skip next 7sts, SC in next 5sts)from*rep x8 [40] **Note:** we have made the holes to form gathers in the next round (pic 3)

Rd 22	**Note:** In the following round, please fold the edges that resulted in the holes forming gathers on the torque and work SC inserting your hook through all layers to fix the gathers (pic 4-5): SC in each st around [40]

Rd 23	Grab the Additional detail that was made on Step 1 and place it inside of the hat (this detail will prevent the stuffing from moving up when we will be stuffing the body). Work SC inserting your hook through both layers and stitching the hat and additional detail together: SC in each st around [40] Pic. 6-7

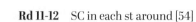

Rd 24-25	SC in each st around [40]
Rd 26	*(SC in next 9sts, INC in next st)from*rep x4 [44]
Rd 27	SC in each st around [44]
Rd 28	*(SC in next 5sts, INC in next st, SC in next 5sts) from*rep x4 [48] Change to Wheat in last st. Do not cut off White, leave it on WS

Continue - BODY
(work in continuous rounds)
(starting the round count from Rd 1 for easier Rd tracking)

Rd 1	**Wheat:** SC BLO in each st around [48]
	Note: we will crochet a hat brim onto these stitches later on Step 4
Rd 2	SC in next 20sts, SC BLO in next 8sts (a nose with mustaches will be attached to these stitches FLO) SC in next 20sts [48]

Rd 3	SC in each st around [48] Change to White in last st. Cut off Wheat
Rd 4	**White:** SC BLO in next 16sts, SC in next 16sts, SC BLO in next st (place a stitch marker #1 into this stitch to mark the point where we will start crocheting a collar), SC BLO in next 15 sts [48]
	Note: into stitches FLO we will work the collar on step 5)
Rd 5	SC in next 10sts, SC BLO in next 4sts (an arm will be attached to these sts), SC in next 20sts, SC BLO in next 4sts an arm will be attached to these sts), SC in next 10sts [48]
Rd 6-9	SC in each st around [48]
Rd 10	*(SC in next 7sts, INC in next st)from*rep x6 [54]

Rd 11-12	SC in each st around [54]
Rd 13	*(SC in next 4sts, INC in next st, SC in next 4sts) from*rep x6 [60]
Rd 14	SC in each st around [60] Change to Bright Green in last st. Cut off White. Place a stitch marker #2 to the last stitch of Rd14 to mark a spot for a hem
Rd 15	**Bright Green:** SC BLO in each st around [60]

Rd 16	*(SC in next 14sts, INC in next st)from*rep x4 [64]
Rd 17-18	SC in each st around [64]
Rd 19	*(SC in next 3sts, SC2tog, SC in next 3sts)from*rep x8 [56]
Rd 20-21	SC in each st around [56]
Rd 22	*(SC in next 5sts, SC2tog) from*rep x8 [48]
Rd 23-24	SC in each st around [48]

Stuff. Stuff as you work

Rd 25	SC BLO in each st around [48]
Rd 26	*(SC in next 2sts, SC2tog, SC in next 2sts)from*rep x8 [40]
Rd 27	*(SC in next 3sts, SC2tog) from*rep x8 [32]
Rd 28	*(SC in next st, SC2tog, SC in next st)from*rep x8 [24]
Rd 29	*(SC in next st, SC2tog) from*rep x8 [16]
	Stuff
Rd 30	SC2tog x8 [8]

Cut off a thread, leave a long tail for sewing. Using this tail and a tapestry needle pull the tail through the last stitches FLO and tighten the opening. Weave in

STEP 4. HAT BRIM
(work in continuous rounds)

Rd 1	Hold the item upside down and join **White** to the last round of the hat: SC FLO in each st around [48]
Rd 2-3	SC in each st around [48]

Cut off a thread and weave in. Pic. 2

STEP 5. COLLAR (work in rows)

Row 1	Hold the item upside down and join **White** to the stitch with the stitch marker #1 placed in Rd 3 of the body: SC FLO in next 32sts [32] Ch1, Turn
Row 2	SC in next 32 sts [32] Pic.3

Cut off a thread and weave in

STEP 6. HEM OF A COAT
(work in continuous rounds)

Rd 1	Hold the item upside down and join **White** to stitch with the marker #2 in Rd 14 of the body and work: SC FLO in each st around [60]
Rd 2	SC in each st around [60] Chage to Melange Black in last st. Cut off White
Rd 3	**Melange Black:** slip stitch BLO in each st around [60]

Cut off a thread and weave in. Pic.4

IMITATION OF A BUTTON PLACKET ON THE COAT

Melange Black: Chain 12

Cut off a thread, leave a long tail for attaching purposes. You can attach this detail now or later by sewing or gluing. Pic 5.

Use Wheat and NOSE pattern on page 110
Use Dark Brown and MUSTACHE pattern on page 110

ARMS (make 2)

Rd 1	**Wheat:** 5SC in magic ring [5] tighten the ring
Rd 2	INC in each st around [10]
Rd 3-5	SC in each st around [10] Change to White in last st. Cut off Wheat

Rd 6-15 White: SC in each st around

Cut off a thread leaving a long tail for attaching purposes

BOOTS (make 2)

Rd 1	**Melange Black:** 6SC in magic ring [6] tighten the ring
Rd 2	INC in each st around [12]
Rd 3	*(SC in next st, INC in next st)from*rep x6 [18]
Rd 4-6	SC in each st around [18]
Rd 7	*(SC in next st, SC2tog) from*rep x6 [12]
	Stuff. Stitch edges together by SC in next 6 stitches inserting your hook through both layers and closing the opening.

Cut off a thread leaving a long tail for attaching purposes.

BERRIES (make 3)

Rd 1	**Red:** 6SC in magic ring [6] tighten the ring

Cut off a thread leaving a long tail for sewing. Using this tail and a tapestry needle pull the tail through the last stitches FLO and tighten the opening. You will need to attach berries to the leaf

LEAF

Bright Green: Chain 8

Row 1	SC in 2nd st from hook, *(hdc in next 2sts, Ch2, sl st in 2nd st from hook, hdc in same st as prev hdc) from*rep x2, hdc in next st, sl st in next st, Ch2, sl st in 2nd st from hook, *(hdc in next 2sts, Ch2, sl st in 2nd st from hook, hdc in same st as prev hdc) from*rep x2, hdc in next st, SC in next st, sl st in next st.

Cut off a thread leaving a long tail for attaching purposes. Scan QR code to watch the video "Christmas Leaves"

ASSEMBLING

Attach the imitation button placket to the coat by sewing it on using the long tail. Alternatively, you can also use glue to fix it in place.

Attach the mustache to the nose

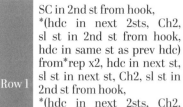

Sew the nose on the body under the hat brim in front to 8 stitches FLO of Rd 1 of the body.

Sew the arms on the body under the hat brim in front to 5 stitches FLO of Rd 4 on both sides.

Hold the body upside down and sew the boots on the body to stitches FLO of Rd 24 on both sides.

LADLE

STEP 1. CHOCOLATE ON A LADLE

Rd 1	**Dark Brown:** 7SC in magic ring [7] tighten the ring
Rd 2	INC in each st around [14]
Rd 3	*(SC in next st, INC in next st)from*rep x7 [21]
Rd 4	*(SC in next st, INC in next st, SC in next st)from*rep x7 [28]
Rd 5	*(SC in next 3sts, INC in next st)from*rep x7 [35]
Rd 6	SC in next st, (make drips) Ch3, hdc in 2nd st from hook, sl st in next ch, SC in next st of the edge(1st drip), hdc in next 3sts, SC in next st, *(Ch4, hdc in 2nd st from hook, sl st in next 2ch, SC in next 2sts of the edge)from*rep x2 (2nd and 3rd drips), Ch5, hdc in 2nd st from hook, sl st in next 3ch, SC in next 2sts of the edge (4th drip), hdc in next 2sts, SC in next st, sl st in next st, SC in next st, hdc in next st, 4DC in next st, hdc in next st, SC in next 2sts, hdc in next 4sts, SC in next st, sl st in next st, SC

Cut off a thread leaving a long tail for attaching purposes if you are going to sew it (or glue).

Attach the leaf with berries to the hat (sew or glue)

Sew or glue 4 buttons or beads to imitate real buttons.

STEP 2. BOWL

Rd 1	**Light Grey:** 7SC in magic ring [7] tighten the ring
Rd 2	INC in each st around [14]
Rd 3	*(SC in next st, INC in next st)from*rep x7 [21]

Rd 4	*(SC in next st, INC in next st, SC in next st)from*rep x7 [28]
Rd 5	*(SC in next 3sts, INC in next st)from*rep x7 [35]
Rd 6	*(SC in next 2sts, INC in next st, SC in next 2sts) from*rep x7 [42]
Rd 7-12	SC in each st around [42]
Rd 13	SC **BLO** in each st around [42]
Rd 14-16	SC in each st around [42]

Take the brown piece you made in step 1 and sew or glue it to the ladle

Rd 17	*(SC in next 2sts, SC2tog, SC in next 2sts)from*rep x7 [35]
Rd 18	*(SC in next 3sts, SC2tog) from*rep x7 [28]
Rd 19	*(SC in next st, SC2tog, SC in next st)from*rep x7 [21]

| Rd 20 | *(SC in next st, SC2tog) from*rep x7 [14] |
| Rd 21 | SC2tog x7 [7] |

Cut off a thread, leave a long tail for sewing and attaching purposes. Using this tail and a tapestry needle sew pull the tail through the last stitches FLO and tighten the opening. Bend the part inward along the 12th round.

STEP 3. SPOON EDGE:

| Rd 1 | With **Light Grey** crochet 1 round of SC FLO along the edge where the fold passes. Cut off a thread and weave in: SC FLO in each st around [42] Pic.below |

STEP 4. HANDLE

| Rd 1 | **Light Grey:** 6SC in magic ring [6] tighten the ring |
| Rd 2-40 | SC in each st around [6] |

Insert a wooden stick into the handle and securely sew up the hole. Cut the thread, leaving the end for future sewing needs. Attach the stick to the bowl by sewing or gluing it in place

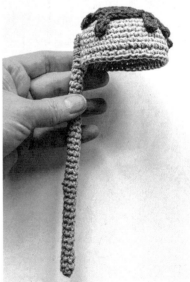

Gingerbread Cookies

SIZE: 30cm/ 11.8in

COLORS AND YARN			TOTAL FOR A PROJECT
Off-white		Yarn Art Jeans 03	Approx. 15g/48meters
Honey caramel		Yarn Art Jeans 07	Approx. 15g/48meters
White		Yarn Art Jeans 62	Approx. 10g/35meters
Wheat		Yarn Art Jeans 05	Approx. 5g/16meters
Dark Brown		Yarn Art Jeans 70	Approx. 25g/80meters

TOOLS
Crochet Hook 2.5mm; Tapestry needle

OTHER MATERIALS
Stuffing approx.50g

CROCHET STITCHES: St(s), Ch, SC, INC, sl st, hdc, DC, SC2tog, FLO, BLO, surface slip stitch

To effectively mark the beginning of each round, it is recommended to use a contrasting thread. This thread should be kept in place until your work is completed.

STEP 1. HAT
(work in continuous rounds)

Rd 1	**Off-white:** 6SC in magic ring [6] tighten the ring. Mark beg of rd in each rd.
Rd 2	SC in each st around [6]
Rd 3	*(INC in next st, SC in next st)from*rep x3[9]
Rd 4	SC in each st around [9]
Rd 5	*(SC in next st, INC in next st, SC in next st) from*rep x3 [12]
Rd 6-7	SC in each st around [12]
Rd 8	*(SC in next 3sts, INC in next st)from*rep x3 [15]
Rd 9-11	SC in each st around [15]
Rd 12	*(SC in next 2sts, INC in next st, SC in next 2sts) from*rep x3 [18]
Rd 13-14	SC in each st around [18]
Rd 15	*(SC in next 5sts, INC in next st)from*rep x3 [21]
Rd 16-17	SC in each st around [21]
Rd 18	*(SC in next 3sts, INC in next st, SC in next 3sts) from*rep x3 [24]
Rd 19-20	SC in each st around [24]
Rd 21	*(SC in next 7sts, INC in next st)from*rep x3 [27] Change to Dark Brown in last st. Cut off Off-white
Rd 22	**Dark Brown:** SC BLO in each st around [27] Note: we will work drips into these sts FLO later
Rd 23	SC in each st around [27]
Rd 24	*(SC in next 4sts, INC in next st, SC in next 4sts) from*rep x3 [30]
Rd 25-26	SC in each st around [30]
Rd 27	*(SC in next 9sts, INC in next st)from*rep x3 [33]

Rd 28-29	SC in each st around [33]
Rd 30	*(SC in next 5sts, INC in next st, SC in next 5sts) from*rep x3 [36]
Rd 31	SC BLO in each st around [36] Note: we will work the decoration #2 into these sts FLO later
Rd 32	SC in each st around [36]
Rd 33	*(SC in next 11sts, INC in next st)from*rep x3 [39]
Rd 34-35	SC in each st around [39]

Rd 36	*(SC in next 6sts, INC in next st, SC in next 6sts) from*rep x3 [42] (Place a stitch marker into the first stitch of this round to makr the starting stitch for «Zigzag» and the decoration #5)
Rd 37	SC BLO in each st around [42]
Rd 38	SC in each st around [42]
Rd 39	*(SC in next 13sts, INC in next st)from*rep x3 [45]
Rd 40-41	SC in each st around [45]
Rd 42	*(SC in next 7sts, INC in next st, SC in next 7sts) from*rep x3 [48]
Rd 43	SC BLO in each st around [48]
Rd 44	SC in each st around [48]
Rd 45	*(SC in next 15sts, INC in next st)from*rep x3 [51]
Rd 46-47	SC in each st around [51]
Rd 48	*(SC in next 8sts, INC in next st, SC in next 8sts) from*rep x3 [54]
Rd 49	SC BLO in each st around [54] Note: we will work the decoration #6 into these sts FLO later
Rd 50	SC in each st around [54]

STEP 2. Continue - HAT BRIM

Rd 51	SC FLO in each st around [54]
Rd 52	*(SC in next 4sts, INC in next st, SC in next 4sts) from*rep x6 [60]
Rd 53	*(SC in next 9sts, INC in next st)from*rep x6 [66] Into stitches of this round we will work a decoration #7
Rd 54	Ch2, *(skip next st, (DC, Ch2, DC)all in next st, skip next st) rep to end, sl st in 2nd Ch

Rd 55	Ch2, *(6DC in next 2Ch-space, SC in next Ch-space)from*rep around

Cut off a thread and weave in

STEP 3. BODY
(work in continuous rounds)

Rd 1	Hold the hat upside down and work in stitches BLO of Rd 50 with **Honey caramel:** SC BLO in each st around [54]

Rd 2	SC in next 23sts, SC BLO in next 8sts (a beard will be attached to these sts), SC in next 23 sts [54]

Rd 3	SC in next 12sts, SC BLO in next 4sts (an arm will be attached to these sts), SC in next 22 sts, SC BLO in next 4sts (an arm will be attached to these sts), SC in next 12 sts [54]
Rd 4-8	SC in each st around [54]
Rd 9	*(SC in next 4sts, INC in next st, SC in next 4sts) from*rep x6 [60]

Rd 10-11	SC in each st around [60]
Rd 12	*(SC in next 14sts, INC in next st)from*rep x4 [64]
Rd 13	SC in each st around [64] Change to Dark Brown in last st. Cut off Honey caramel

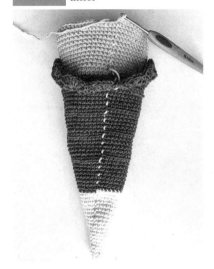

Rd 14	**Dark Brown:** *(SC BLO in next 3sts, SC2tog BLO, SC BLO in next 3sts) from*rep x8 [56]
Rd 15-16	SC in each st around [56]

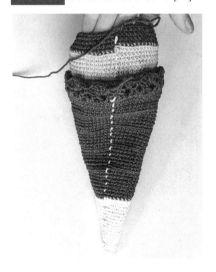

Drop the Dark Brown loop from your hook and make surface slip stitches in between Rd 13 and 14 around with new **Off white**. Cut off thread, weave in

STEP 4. Cream drips
(work in continuous rounds)

Rd 1 Hold the hat upside down and work in stitches BLO of Rd 21 of the step 1 with **Off white** (start from the beginning of rd):
*(INC in next st, SC in next 6sts)from*rep x3, INC in next st, SC in next 5sts [31]

1st drip: Chain 3, hdc in 2nd Ch from hook, hdc in next st of chain, hdc in stitch of main part where Ch3 comes from, skip next st of a main part, SC in next st of main part
2nd drip: Chain 4, hdc in 2nd Ch from hook, hdc in next 2sts of chain, hdc in stitch of main part where Ch4 comes from, skip next st of a main part, SC in next st of main part
3rd drip: Chain 5, hdc in 2nd Ch from hook, hdc in next 3sts of chain, hdc in stitch of main part where Ch5 comes from, skip next st of a main part, SC in next 2sts of main part
4th drip: skip next st, 5DC in next st, skip next st, SC in next 2sts,
5th drip: Chain 3, hdc in 2nd Ch from hook, hdc in next st of chain, hdc in stitch of main part where Ch3 comes from, skip next st of a main part, SC in next st of main part
Rd 2 **6th drip**: Chain 4, hdc in 2nd Ch from hook, hdc in next 2sts of chain, hdc in stitch of main part where Ch4 comes from, skip next st of a main part, SC in next 2sts of main part
7th drip: skip next st, 5DC in next st, skip next st, SC in next st,
8th drip: Chain 3, hdc in 2nd Ch from hook, hdc in next st of chain, hdc in stitch of main part where Ch3 comes from, skip next st of a main part, SC in next st of main part
9th drip: Chain 4, hdc in 2nd Ch from hook, hdc in next 2sts of chain, hdc in stitch of main part where Ch4 comes from, skip next st of a main part, SC in next 2sts of main part
10th drip: skip next st, 5DC in next st, skip next st, SC in next st, sl st in next st

Cut off a thread and weave in or leave a long tail and use it later for attaching the edge to the surface.

Rd 17	Grab **Dark Brown** back on your hook and continue working: *(SC in next 5sts, SC2tog)from*rep x8 [48]
Rd 18	SC in each st around [48]

Stuff. Stuff as you work

Rd 19	SC BLO in each st around [48]
Rd 20	*(SC in next 2sts, SC2tog, SC in next 2sts)from*rep x8 [40]
Rd 21	*(SC in next 3sts, SC2tog) from*rep x8 [32]
Rd 22	*(SC in next st, SC2tog, SC in next st)from*rep x8 [24]
Rd 23	*(SC in next st, SC2tog) from*rep x8 [16]
Rd 24	SC2tog x8 [8]

Cut off a thread, leave a long tail for sewing. Thread the tapestry needle with the tail and pull it through the FLO of the stitches on the last round and tighten. Weave in

STEP 5. DECORATIONS

Hold the item upside down when working decorations

#1 Work in stitches BLO of Rd 55 of the step 2 with **Off white** (start from the beg of rd): surface sl st in each st around. Cut off a thread and weave in

#2 Work in stitches BLO of Rd 30 of the step 1 with **Off white** (start from the beg of rd): *(skip next st, all in next st [3DC, Ch2, sl st in top of previous DC, 3DC], skip next st, SC in next st) from*rep x9 [9 shells]

Scan to watch a video tutorial "Crochet" in top of a stitch"

#3 With **Off white** work surface slip stitches in stitches of Rd 30 of step 1. Weave in

#4 Join **Off white** to stitch with the stitch marker (Rd 36): *(Ch5, SC FLO in next 6th st of rd 42, Ch5, SC FLO in next 5th st of rd 36) from*rep around. Weave in

#5 With **Off white** work surface slip stitches in stitches of Rd 36. Weave in

#6 With **Off white** work surface slip stitches in stitches of Rd 49. Weave in

#7 With **Off white** work in stitches of Rd 53: *(Ch4, SC in same st as [DC, Ch2, DC] of Rd 54 inserting your hook in between two DC)from*rep around. Weave in

STARS (make 4)

Rd 1 **Off white:** 10SC in magic ring [10] tighten the ring

Rd 2 *(Ch3, sl st in 2nd st from hook, hdc in next ch, skip next st of Rd 1, sl st in next st of Rd1) from*rep x5

Cut off a thread leaving a long tail for attaching purposes

HEARTS (make 4)

Rd 1 **Off white:** Make a magic ring and work in ring: SC, hdc, 5DC, Ch2, 5DC, hdc, SC, tighten the ring

Cut off a thread leaving a long tail for attaching purposes

Attach the stars and hearts to the body

Use Wheat and
NOSE pattern on page 110

Use White and BEARD
pattern #2 on page 110

ARMS (make 2)
(WORK IN CONTINUOUS ROUNDS)

STEP 1. ARM

Rd 1	**Wheat:** 5SC in magic ring [5] tighten the ring
Rd 2	INC in each st around [10]
Rd 3-5	SC in each st around [10] Change to **Off-White** in last st. Cut off Honey Caramel
Rd 6-7	**Honey caramel:** SC in each st around [10]
Rd 8	SC BLO in each st around [10]
Rd 9-15	SC in each st around [10]

Cut off a thread leaving a long tail for attaching purposes.

STEP 2. CUFF

Rd 1	**Dark Brown:** Hold the arm upside-down and work into stitches FLO of Rd 7: SC FLO in each st around [10]
Rd 2	SC in each st around [10]

Cut off a thread and weave in

ASSEMBLING

Sew the nose on the beard.

Attach the beard with the nose on the body under the hat brim (Rd 2 of the body)

Sew the hands on the body under the hat brim

Christmas Guard

SIZE: 19cm/ 7.5in

COLORS AND YARN			TOTAL FOR A PROJECT
Wheat		Yarn Art Jeans 05	Approx. 10g/35meters
White		Yarn Art Jeans 62	Approx. 5g/16meters
Red		Yarn Art Jeans 90	Approx. 15g/50meters
Melange Black		Yarn Art Jeans 28	Approx. 25g/80meters
Bright Yellow		Yarn Art Jeans 35	A little amount
Gold metallic yarn		DROPS Glitter	A little amount(optional)

TOOLS
Crochet Hook 2.5mm; Tapestry needle; Stitch markers

OTHER MATERIALS
Stuffing approx. 40g

CROCHET STITCHES:
St(s), Ch, SC, INC, sl st, hdc, SC2tog, FLO, BLO

To effectively mark the beginning of each round, it is recommended to use a contrasting thread. This thread should be kept in place until your work is completed.

STEP 1. HAT
(work in continuous rounds)

Rd 1	**Melange Black:** 6SC in magic ring [6] tighten the ring. Mark beg of rd in each rd
Rd 2	INC in each st around [12]
Rd 3	*(SC in next st, INC in next st)from*rep x6 [18]
Rd 4	*(SC in next st, INC in next st, SC in next st)from*rep x6 [24]
Rd 5	*(SC in next 3sts, INC in next st)from*rep x6 [30]
Rd 6	*(SC in next 2sts, INC in next st, SC in next 2sts)from*rep x6 [36]
Rd 7	*(SC in next 5sts, INC in next st)from*rep x6 [42]
Rd 8	*(SC in next 3sts, INC in next st, SC in next 3sts)from*rep x6
Rd 9	SC in each st around [48]
Rd 10	*(SC in next 7sts, INC in next st)from*rep x6 [54]
Rd 11-24	SC in each st around [54]
Rd 25	*(SC BLO in next 7sts, SC-2tog BLO)from*rep x6 [48] Place a stitch marker into the last st of this rd. **Note:** we will crochet a hat brim on these stitches FLO
Rd 26-27	SC in each st around [48] Change to Wheat in last st. Cut off Melange Black

STEP 2. Continue - BODY
(work in continuous rounds)

Rd 28	**Wheat:** SC in each st around [48]

Rd 29	SC in next 22sts, SC BLO in next 4sts (a nose will be attached to these sts), SC in next 22sts [48]
Rd 30	SC in each st around [48] Change to Red in last st. Cut off Wheat
Rd 31	**Red:** SC in each st around [48]

Rd 32	SC in next 10sts, SC BLO in next 4sts (an arm will be attached to these sts), SC in next 20sts, SC BLO in next 4sts (n arm will be attached to these sts), SC in next 10sts [48]
Rd 33-36	SC in each st around [48]
Rd 37	*(SC in next 7sts, INC in next st)from*rep x6 [54]
Rd 38-39	SC in each st around [54]
Rd 40	*(SC in next 4sts, INC in next st, SC in next 4sts) from*rep x6 [60]
Rd 41	SC in each st around [60] Change to Melange Black in last st. Cut off Red

Place a stitch marker #2 to the last stitch of Rd 14 to mark a belt

Rd 42	**Melange Black:** SC BLO in each st around [60]
Rd 43	*(SC in next 14sts, INC in next st)from*rep x4 [64]

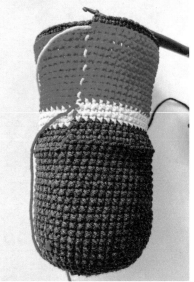

Rd 44-45	SC in each st around [64]
Rd 46	*(SC in next 3sts, SC2tog, SC in next 3sts) from*rep x8 [56]
Rd 47-48	SC in each st around [56]
Rd 49	*(SC in next 5sts, SC2tog) from*rep x8 [48]
Rd 50-51	SC in each st around [48]
Rd 52	SC BLO in each st around [48] **Note:** the boots will be attached to these stitches FLO
Rd 53	*(SC in next 2sts, SC2tog, SC in next 2sts) from*rep x8 [40]

Stuff. Stuff as you work

Rd 54	*(SC in next 3sts, SC2tog) from*rep x8 [32]
Rd 55	*(SC in next st, SC2tog, SC in next st)from*rep x8 [24]
Rd 56	*(SC in next st, SC2tog) from*rep x8 [16]
	Stuff
Rd 57	SC2tog x8 [8]

Cut off a thread, leave a long tail for sewing. Using this tail and a tapestry needle pull the tail through the last stitches flo and tighten the opening. Weave in

STEP 3. HAT BRIM

| Rd 1 | Hold the item upside down and join **Melange Black** to the stitch with the marker #1 (Rd 24-hat) and work: SC FLO in each st around [54] |

| Rd 2 | SC in each st around [54] |

From the next round we're going to work in joined rounds

Rd 3	Ch2, hdc in next 15sts, SC in next 24sts, hdc in next 14sts, sl st in 2nd Ch to join rd [54]
Rd 4	Ch2, hdc in next 17sts (place a stitch marker into the stitch leg of 17th hdc on right side), SC in next 20sts, hdc in next st (place a stitch marker into the stitch leg of this hdc on right side), hdc in next 15sts, sl st in 2nd Ch to join rd [54] **Note:** we marked the points where the chained straps will be attached
Rd 5	Ch2, hdc in each st around, sl st in 2nd Ch to join rd [54]

Cut off a thread and weave in

STEP 4. HEM ON THE RED TUNIC

| Rd 1 | Hold the item upside down and join **Red** to the stitch with the marker #2: SC FLO in each st around [60] |
| Rd 2 | SC in each st around [60] |

Cut off a thread and weave in

IMITATION OF A BUTTON PLACKET ON THE TUNIC

White: Chain 12

Cut off a thread, leave a long tail for attaching purposes (we will fix this chain later as shown in pic.below).

BELT

White: Chain 62

Row 1   hdc in 3th stitch from hook, hdc in each st across [60]

Cut off a thread, leave a long tail for attaching purposes.

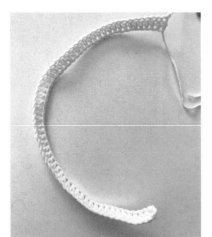

BOOTS (make 2)

(work in continuous rounds)

Rd 1	**Melange Black:** 6SC in magic ring [6] tighten the ring
Rd 2	INC in each st around [12]
Rd 3	*(SC in next st, INC in next st)from*rep x6 [18]
Rd 4-6	SC in each st around [18]
Rd 7	*(SC in next st, SC2tog) from*rep x6 [12]
	Stuff. Stitch edges together by SC in next 6 stitches inserting your hook through both layers and closing the opening.

Cut off a thread leaving a long tail for attaching purposes.

ARMS (make 2)
(work in continuous rounds)

STEP 1. ARM

Rd 1	**Wheat:** 5SC in magic ring [5] tighten the ring
Rd 2	INC in each st around [10]
Rd 3-5	SC in each st around [10] Change to Red in last st. Cut off Wheat
Rd 6-7	**Red:** SC in each st around [10]
Rd 8	SC BLO in each st around [10]
Rd 9-17	SC in each st around [10]

Cut off a thread leaving a long tail for attaching purposes

STEP 2. CUFF

Rd 1	Hold the arm upside down and with **Melange Black** work into stitches FLO of Rd 7: SC FLO in each st around [10]
Rd 2	SC in each st around [10]

Cut off a thread and weave in

Use Wheat and the NOSE pattern on page 110

Scan to watch a video tutorial "Chained strap

CHAINED STRAP

Rd 1	**Bright Yellow** + Gold metallic yarn: *(Ch1, hdc in bottom loop of Ch)from*repeat x15

Bottom loop

Bottom loop

ASSEMBLING

1.Locate 8 stitches FLO under the hat brim in front make to attach the nose. Sew or glue the white chain(the button placket) onto the body, positioning it in the middle of these stitches nose

2. Sew or glue the nose to 4 stitches FLO of Rd 28 of the body under the hat brim.

3. Sew or glue the white belt to the waist and with Yellow+Gold metalic yarn embroider a frame buckle

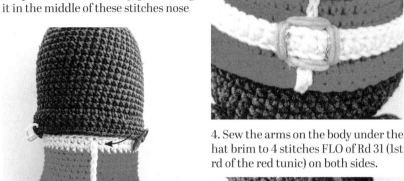

4. Sew the arms on the body under the hat brim to 4 stitches FLO of Rd 31 (1st rd of the red tunic) on both sides.

5. Hold the gnome upside down and sew the boots on the body to stitches FLO of Rd 51 on both sides.

6. Sew or glue the chain on the hat brim to the stitch markers

Bell Gnome

SIZE: 18cm/ 7in

COLORS AND YARN | TOTAL FOR A PROJECT

Color		Yarn	Total
Red	⭐	Yarn Art Jeans 90	Approx. 10g/35meters
Wheat	⭐	Yarn Art Jeans 05	Approx. 5g/15meters
Bright Yellow	⭐	Yarn Art Jeans 35	Approx. 15g/48meters
Bright Green	⭐	Yarn Art Jeans 52	Approx. 20g/70meters
White	☆	Yarn Art Jeans 62	Approx. 3g/10meters
Brown	⭐	Yarn Art Jeans 40	Approx. 3g/10meters

TOOLS
Crochet Hook 2.5mm; Tapestry needle

OTHER MATERIALS
Stuffing approx. 40g

CROCHET STITCHES:
St(s), Ch, hdc, SC, DC, INC, sl st, SC2tog

BOW (WORK IN ROWS)

STEP 1. MAIN DETAIL

	Red: Chain 41 [41]
Row 1	SC in 2nd st from hook, SC in next 39sts [40], Ch1, Turn
Row 2-5	SC in each st across [40], Ch1, Turn
Row 6	SC in each st across [40]

Cut off a thread, leave a long tail for sewing. Sew into a ring and tie in the middle

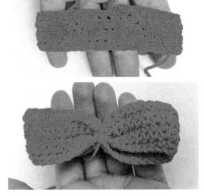

STEP 2. ADDITIONAL DETAIL

	Red: Chain 17
Row 1	SC in 2nd st from hook, SC in next 15 sts [16], Ch1, Turn
Row 2	INC in next st, SC in next 14sts, INC in last st [18], Ch1, Turn
Row 3	INC in next st, SC in next 16sts, INC in last st [20], Ch1, Turn
Row 4	INC in next st, SC in next 18sts, INC in last st [22], Ch1, Turn
Row 5	INC in next st, SC in next 20sts, INC in last st [24], Ch1, Turn
Row 6	INC in next st, SC in next 22sts, INC in last st [26]

Cut off a thread and weave in ends. Take a red thread and wrap it around the center of this detail.

STEP 3. RING

	Red: Chain 11
Row 1	SC in 2nd st from hook, SC in next 9sts [10], Ch1, Turn
Row 2	SC in each st across [10], Ch1, Turn
Row 3	SC in each st across [10]

Cut off a thread, leave a long tail for sewing.

Arrange all details together and Wrap the middle of the bow with this detail and stitch edges together.

HAT

STEP 1. LOOP ON A BELL

	Bright Yellow Chain 25
Row 1	sl st in 2nd st from hook, sl st in next 23sts [24]

Cut off a thread, leave a long tail for attaching purposes.

To effectively mark the beginning of each round, it is recommended to use a contrasting thread. This thread should be kept in place until your work is completed.

STEP 2. HAT
(work in continuous rounds)

Rd 1	**Bright Yellow:** 6SC in magic ring [6] tighten the ring
Rd 2	INC in each st around [12]
Rd 3	*(SC in next st, INC in next st)from*rep x6 [18]
Rd 4	*(SC in next st, INC in next st, SC in next st) from*rep x6 [24]
Rd 5	*(SC in next 3sts, INC in next st)from*rep x6[30]
Rd 6	*(SC in next 2sts, INC in next st, SC in next 2sts) from*rep x6 [36]
Rd 7-9	SC in each st around [36]
Rd 10	*(SC in next 11sts, INC in next st) from*rep **x3** [39]
Rd 11	SC in each st around [39]
Rd 12	*(SC in next 6sts, INC in next st, SC in next 6sts) from*rep x3 [42]
Rd 13-15	SC in each st around [42]
Rd 16	*(SC in next 13sts, INC in next st)from*rep x3 [45]
Rd 17-18	SC in each st around [45]
Rd 19	*(SC in next 7sts, INC in next st, SC in next 7sts) from*rep x3 [48]
Rd 20	SC in each st around [48]

STEP 2. HAT BRIM

Rd 21	SC FLO in each st around [48]
Rd 22	*(SC in next 7sts, INC in next st) from*rep x6 [54]
Rd 23	*(SC in next 4sts, INC in next st, SC in next 4sts) from*rep x6 [60]
Rd 24	*(SC in next 9sts, INC in next st)from*rep x6 [66]
Rd 25	sl st in each st around [66]

Cut off Bright Yellow. Sew the loop on the top of the bow. Attach the bow on the hat when you have done Rd 2 and locate the face side or do that later.

BODY
(work in continuous rounds)

Rd 1	Hold the hat upside down and with **Bright Green** work into stitches BLO of Rd 20: SC BLO in each st around [48]

Rd 2	SC in next 20sts, SC BLO in next 8sts (a nose will be attached to these sts), SC in next 20sts [48]
Rd 3	SC in next 10 sts, SC BLO in next 4 sts (an arm will be attached to these sts), SC in next 20sts, SC BLO in next 4 sts (an arm will be attached to these sts), SC in next 10 sts [48]
Rd 4-7	SC in each st around [48]

Rd 8	*(SC in next 11sts, INC in next st)from*rep x4[52]
Rd 9	SC in each st around [52]
Rd 10	*(SC in next 6sts, INC in next st, SC in next 6sts) from*rep x4 [56]
Rd 11	SC in each st around [56]
Rd 12	*(SC in next 6sts, INC in next st)from*rep x8 [64]
Rd 13	SC in each st around [64] Note: place a stitch maker into the 1st st of this round to mark the spot where we will start crocheting a Two-colored braid
Rd 14	SC BLO in each st around [64] Note: we will crochet a braid into these sts FLO later
Rd 15-16	SC in each st around [64]
Rd 17	*(SC in next 3sts, SC2tog, SC in next 3sts)from*rep x8 [56]
Rd 18	SC in each st around [48]
Rd 19	*(SC in next 5sts, SC2tog) from*rep x8 [48]
	Stuff. Stuff as you work
Rd 20-21	SC in each st around [48]
Rd 22	SC BLO in each st around [48]
Rd 23	*(SC in next 2sts, SC2tog, SC in next 2sts)from*rep x8 [40]
Rd 24	*(SC in next 3sts, SC2tog) from*rep x8 [32]
Rd 25	*(SC in next st, SC2tog, SC in next st)from*rep x8[24]
Rd 26	*(SC in next st, SC2tog) from*rep x8 [16]
Rd 27	SC2tog x8 [8]

Cut off a thread, leave a long tail for sewing. Using this tail and a tapestry needle sew pull the tail through the last stitches flo and tighten the opening.

STAND

Rd 1	Hold the gnome upside down and with **Brown** work into stitches FLO of Rd 21 of the body: Ch1, hdc FLO in each st around [48] Cut off and weave in

TWO-COLORED BRAID

Use Off-White and Red, follow the pattern on page 25 (Poinsettia).

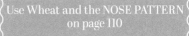

Use Wheat and the NOSE PATTERN on page 110

ARMS (make 2)
(work in continuous rounds)

Rd 1	**Wheat:** 5SC in magic ring [5] tighten the ring
Rd 2	INC in each st around [10]
Rd 3-5	SC in each st around [10] Change to Bright green in last st. Cut off Wheat
Rd 6-15	**Bright Green:** SC in each st around [10]

Cut off thread leaving a long tail for attaching purposes

ASSEMBLING

Sew the nose on the body under the hat brim in front to 8 stitches FLO of Rd 1 of the body. Sew the arms on the body under the hat brim to 4 stitches FLO of Rd 2 of the body on both sides.

**SIZE:
24cm/
9.5in**

COLORS AND YARN

TOTAL FOR A PROJECT

Bright Yellow		Yarn Art Jeans 35	Approx. 15g/48meters
White		Yarn Art Jeans 62	Approx. 12g/40meters
Honey caramel		Yarn Art Jeans 07	Approx. 15g/48meters
Red		Yarn Art Jeans 90	Approx. 7g/22meters
Wheat		Yarn Art Jeans 05	Approx. 5g/16meters

FOR CANDIES

Blue		Yarn Art Jeans 76	A little amount
Coral		Yarn Art Jeans 23	A little amount
Light Green		Yarn Art Jeans 29	A little amount
Rose pink		Yarn Art Jeans 20	A little amount

TOOLS
Crochet Hook 2.5mm
Tapestry needles

OTHER MATERIALS
Stuffing approx.50g

CROCHET STITCHES:
St(s), Ch, hdc, SC, DC,
INC, SC2tog

To effectively mark the beginning of each round, it is recommended to use a contrasting thread. This thread should be kept in place until your work is completed

STEP 1. HAT
(work in continuous rounds)

Rd 1	**White:** 6SC in magic ring (Change to Bright Yellow in last s)[6] tighten the ring. Mark beg of rd in each rd

Now we are going to work in tapestry crochet technique (when we change colors and carry a non-working color inside of stitches, see page 5)

Rd 2	Alternate 1x **Bright Yellow** st and 1x **White** st: SC in each st around [12]
Rd 3	(**Bright Yellow:** SC in next Bright Yellow st, **White:** SC in next White st) rep to end [12]
Rd 4	*(**Bright Yellow:** SC in next Bright Yellow st, **White:** INC in next White st) from*rep x6[18]
Rd 5-6	*(**Bright Yellow:** SC in next Bright Yellow st, **White:** SC in next White 2sts) from*rep x6 [18]
Rd 7	*(**Bright Yellow:** SC in next Bright Yellow st, **White:** INC in next White st, SC in next White st) from*rep x6 [24]
Rd 8-9	*(**Bright Yellow:** SC in next Bright Yellow st, **White:** SC in next White 3sts)from*rep x6 [24]
Rd 10	*(**Bright Yellow:** INC in next Bright Yellow st, **White:** SC in next White 3sts)from*rep x6 [30]
Rd 11-12	*(**Bright Yellow:** SC in next Bright Yellow 2sts, **White:** SC in next White 3sts)from*rep x6 [30]
Rd 13	*(**Bright Yellow:** INC in next Bright Yellow st, SC in next Bright Yellow st, **White:** SC in next White 3sts)from*rep x6 [36]

Rd 14-15	*(**Bright Yellow:** SC in next Bright Yellow 3sts, **White:** SC in next White 3sts) from*rep x6 [36]

Rd 16	*(**Bright Yellow:** SC in next Bright Yellow 3sts, **White:** INC in next White st, **Bright Yellow:** SC in next White st, **White:** SC in next White st)from*rep x6 [42]
Rd 17-18	*(**Bright Yellow:** SC in next Bright Yellow 3sts, **White:** SC in next White 2sts, **Bright Yellow:** SC in next Bright Yellow st, **White:** SC in next White st)from*rep x6 [42]
Rd 19	*(**Bright Yellow:** SC in next Bright Yellow 3sts, **White:** SC in next White 2sts, **Bright Yellow:** SC in next Bright Yellow st, **White:** INC in next White st)from*rep x6 [48]
Rd 20-21	*(**Bright Yellow:** SC in next Bright Yellow 3sts, **White:** SC in next White 2sts, **Bright Yellow:** SC in next Bright Yellow st, **White:** SC in next White 2sts)from*rep x6 [48]
Rd 22	*(**Bright Yellow:** SC in next Bright Yellow 3sts, **White:** SC in next White 2sts, **Bright Yellow:** INC in next Bright Yellow st, **White:** SC in next White 2sts)from*rep x6 [54]

Rd 23-24	*(**Bright Yellow:** SC in next Bright Yellow 3sts, **White:** SC in next White 2sts, **Bright Yellow:** SC in next Bright Yellow 2sts, **White:** SC in next White 2sts)from*rep x6 [54] (in pic. 23rd rd)

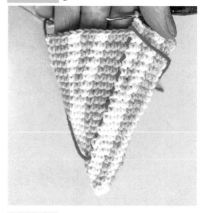

Rd 25	*(**Bright Yellow:** SC in next Bright Yellow 3sts, **White:** INC in next White st, SC in next White st, **Bright Yellow:** SC in next Bright Yellow 2sts, **White:** SC in next White 2sts) from*rep x6 [60]
Rd 26-27	*(**Bright Yellow:** SC in next Bright Yellow 3sts, **White:** SC in next White 3sts, **Bright Yellow:** SC in next Bright Yellow 2sts, **White:** SC in next White 2sts)from*rep x6 [60]
Rd 28	*(**Bright Yellow:** SC in next Bright Yellow 3sts, **White:** SC in next White 3sts, **Bright Yellow:** INC in next Bright Yellow st, SC in next Bright Yellow st, **White:** SC in next White 2sts)from*rep x6 [66]
Rd 29-30	*(**Bright Yellow:** SC in next Bright Yellow 3sts, **White:** SC in next White 3sts, **Bright Yellow:** SC in next Bright Yellow 3sts, **White:** SC in next White 2sts) from*rep x6 [66]

Continue - HAT BRIM

Rd 31

Work this round FLO: *(**Bright Yellow:** SC in next Bright Yellow 3sts, **White:** SC in next White 3sts, **Bright Yellow:** SC in next Bright Yellow 3sts, **White:** SC in next White 2sts)from*rep x6 [66]

Rd 32

*(**Bright Yellow:** SC in next Bright Yellow 3sts, **White:** SC in next White 3sts, **Bright Yellow:** SC in next Bright Yellow 3sts, **White:** SC in next White st, INC in next White st) from*rep x6 [72]

Rd 33

*(**Bright Yellow:** SC in next Bright Yellow 3sts, **White:** SC in next White 3sts)from*rep x12 [72]

Rd 34

*(**Bright Yellow:** 2DC in next Bright Yellow 3sts, **White:** skip White st, SC in next White st, skip White st)from*rep x12

Cut off a thread and weave in

Use Red and the pompon pattern on page 111

STEP 2. BODY

Rd 1

Hold the hat upside down and work in stitches BLO of Rd 30 with **Honey caramel**: SC BLO in each st around [66]

Rd 2

SC in next 15sts, SC BLO in next 4sts(an arm will be attached to these sts), SC in next 10sts, SC BLO in next 8sts (a beard will be attached to these sts), SC in next 10sts, SC BLO in next 4sts (an arm will be attached to these sts), SC in next 15sts [66]

Rd 3-7 — SC in each st around [66]

Sew the pompon on the top of the hat or glue it on later

Rd 8 — *(SC in next 9sts, SC2tog) from*rep x6 [60]

Rd 9-10 — SC in each st around [60]

Rd 11 — *(SC in next 4sts, SC2tog, SC in next 4sts)from*rep x6 [54]

Rd 12 — SC in each st around [54] Change to Bright yellow in last st. Cut off Honey caramel

Rd 13 — **Bright Yellow:** *(SC BLO in next 7sts, SC2tog BLO) from*rep x6[48]

Rd 14-15 — SC in each st around [48]

Drop the Bright Yellow loop from your hook for a while

Red: work surface slip stitches in between Rd 12 and 13 around. Cut off Red and weave in (see pic 1 on next page)

Stuff. Stuff as you work

Rd 16

Grab the **Bright Yellow** loop back o your hook and continue working: SC BLO in each st around [48]
Note: we will work into these stitches FLO to make a stand later.

Rd 17 — *(SC in next 2sts, SC2tog, SC in next 2sts)from*rep x8 [40]

Rd 18 — *(SC in next 3sts, SC2tog) from*rep x8 [32]

Rd 19 — *(SC in next st, SC2tog, SC in next st)from*rep x8 [24]

Rd 20 — *(SC in next st, SC2tog) from*rep x8 [16]

Rd 21   SC2tog x8 [8]

Cut off a thread, leave a long tail for sewing. Using this tail and a tapestry needle sew pull the tail through the last stitches FLO and tighten the opening. Weave in

Surface slip stitch

Use Wheat and NOSE pattern on page 110

Use White and BEARD pattern #1 on page 110

STEP 4. STAND

Hold the gnome upside down and with Red work into stitch FLO of Rd 15 of the body: Ch1, SC FLO in each st around [48]

Cut off a thread and weave in

CANDIES
(work in continuous rounds)
Make 3x Blue, 2x Coral, 1x Light Green

Rd 1   6SC in magic ring [6] tighten the ring

Rd 2   INC in each st around [12]

Rd 3   SC in each st around [12]

Rd 4   SC2tog x6 [6]

Cut off a thread, leave a long tail for sewing. Using this tail and a tapestry needle sew pull the tail through the last stitches FLO and tighten the opening.

HEARTS make 2

Rd 1   **Off white:** Make a magic ring and work in ring: SC, hdc, 5DC, Ch2, 5DC, hdc, SC, tighten the ring

Cut off thread leaving a long tail for sewing

ARMs (make 2)
(work in continuous rounds)

STEP 1. ARM

Rd 1	**Wheat:** 5SC in magic ring [5] tighten the ring
Rd 2	INC in each st around [10]
Rd 3-5	SC in each st around [10] Change to Honey caramel in last st. Cut off Wheat
Rd 6-7	**Honey caramel:** SC in each st around [10]
Rd 8	SC BLO in each st around [10]
Rd 9-16	SC in each st around [10]

Cut off thread leaving a long tail for attaching purposes

STEP 2. CUFF

| Rd 1 | **Bright Yellow:** work into stitches FLO of Rd 7: SC FLO in each st around [10] |
| Rd 2 | SC in each st around [10] |

Cut off a thread and weave in

ASSEMBLING

Sew the nose on the beard and attach the beard on the stitches FLO of Rd 1 of the body under the hat brim in front.

Sew the arms on the body under the hat brim to 4 stitches FLO of Rd 1 on both sides. Sew or glue the candies on the hat.

SIZE:
24cm/
9.5in

COLORS AND YARN

TOTAL FOR A PROJECT

Color		Yarn	Total
Light Blue		Yarn Art Jeans 75	Approx. 40g/128meters
Wheat		Yarn Art Jeans 05	Approx. 5g/15meters
White		Yarn Art Jeans 62	Approx. 7g/20 meters
Bright Yellow		Yarn Art Jeans 35	Approx. 10g/35meters
Gold metallic yarn		DROPS Glitter	A little amount(optional)
White Fur**		Rico Baby Teddy**	Approx. 10g/25meters (optional)

** You can use any fluffy yarn. I crocheted wings in double strand using one fluffy thread + one white thread of the main yarn. If your the fluffy thread is thick, you can crochet in a single strand

TOOLS
Crochet Hook 2.5mm ;Tapestry needle

OTHER MATERIALS
Stuffing approx. 50g

CROCHET STITCHES:
St(s), Ch, SC, hdc, INC, sl st, SC2tog, FLO, BLO

Angel

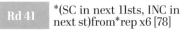

To effectively mark the beginning of each round, it is recommended to use a contrasting thread. This thread should be kept in place until your work is completed.

HAT
(work in continuous rounds)

Rd 1	**Light Blue:** 6SC in magic ring [6] tighten the ring
Rd 2	*(INC in next st, SC in next st)from*rep x3 [9]
Rd 3-5	SC in each st around[9]
Rd 6	*(SC in next st, INC in next st, SC in next st)from*rep x3 [12]
Rd 7-8	SC in each st around [12]
Rd 9	*(SC in next 3sts, INC in next st)from*rep x3 [15]
Rd 10-11	SC in each st around [15]
Rd 12	*(SC in next 2sts, INC in next st, SC in next 2sts)from*rep x3 [18]
Rd 13-14	SC in each st around [18]
Rd 15	*(SC in next 5sts, INC in next st)from*rep x3 [21]
Rd 16	SC in each st around [21]
Rd 17	*(SC in next 3sts, INC in next st, SC in next 3sts)from*rep x3 [24]
Rd 18	SC in each st around [24]
Rd 19	*(SC in next 7sts, INC in next st)from*rep x3 [27]
Rd 20	SC in each st around [27]
Rd 21	*(SC in next 4sts, INC in next st, SC in next 4sts)from*rep x3 [30]
Rd 22	SC in each st around [30]
Rd 23	*(SC in next 9sts, INC in next st)from*rep x3 [33]
Rd 24	SC in each st around [33]
Rd 25	*(SC in next 5sts, INC in next st, SC in next 5sts)from*rep x3 [36]
Rd 26	SC in each st around [36]

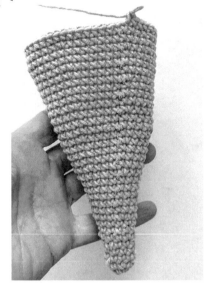

Rd 27	*(SC in next 11sts, INC in next st)from*rep x3 [39]
Rd 28	SC in each st around [39]
Rd 29	*(SC in next 6sts, INC in next st, SC in next 6sts)from*rep x3 [42]
Rd 30	SC in each st around [42]
Rd 31	*(SC in next 13sts, INC in next st)from*rep x3 [45]
Rd 32	SC in each st around [45]
Rd 33	*(SC in next 7sts, INC in next st, SC in next 7sts)from*rep x3 [48]
Rd 34	SC in each st around [48]

CONTINUE - HAT BRIM

Rd 35	*(SC FLO in next 15sts, INC FLO in next st)from*rep x3 [51]
Rd 36	*(SC in next 8sts, INC in next st, SC in next 8sts)from*rep x3 [54]
Rd 37	*(SC in next 4sts, INC in next st, SC in next 4sts)from*rep **x6** [60]
Rd 38	*(SC in next 9sts, INC in next st)from*rep x6 [66]
Rd 39	*(SC in next 5sts, INC in next st, SC in next 5sts)from*rep x6 [72]
Rd 40	SC in each st around [72]

Rd 41	*(SC in next 11sts, INC in next st)from*rep x6 [78]

Cut off a thread and weave in

BODY
(work in continuous rounds)

Rd 1	Hold the hat upside down and with **Light Blue** work into stitches BLO of Rd 34: SC BLO in each st around [48]

Rd 2	SC in next 20sts, SC BLO in next 8sts (a beard will be attached to these sts), SC in next 20sts [48]
Rd 3	SC in next 10sts, SC BLO in next 4sts (an arm will be attached to these sts), SC in next 20sts, SC BLO in next 4sts (an arm will be attached to these sts), SC in next 10sts [48]
Rd 4-9	SC in each st around [48]
Rd 10	*(SC in next 5sts, INC in next st)from*rep x8 [56]
Rd 11-13	SC in each st around [56]
Rd 14	*(SC in next 3sts, INC in next st, SC in next 3sts) from*rep x8 [64]
Rd 15-17	SC in each st around [64]
Rd 18	*(SC in next 3sts, SC2tog, SC in next 3sts)from*rep x8 [56]
Rd 19-20	SC in each st around [56]
Rd 21	*(SC in next 5sts, SC2tog) from*rep x8 [48]
	Stuff. Stuff as you work
Rd 22-23	SC in each st around [48]
Rd 24	SC BLO in each st around [48]
Rd 25	*(SC in next 2sts, SC2tog, SC in next 2sts)from*rep x8 [40]
Rd 26	*(SC in next 3sts, SC2tog) from*rep x8 [32]
Rd 27	*(SC in next st, SC2tog, SC in next st)from*rep x8 [24]
Rd 28	*(SC in next st, SC2tog) from*rep x8 [16]
	Stuff
Rd 229	SC2tog x8 [8]

Cut off a thread, leave a long tail for sewing. Using this tail and a tapestry needle pull the tail through the last stitches FLO and tighten the opening. Weave in

Use Wheat and NOSE pattern on page 110
Use White and BEARD pattern #2 on page 110

HAIR (WORK IN ROWS)

Bright Yellow: Chain 49

Row 1	SC in 2nd st from hook, SC in each st around [48] Ch1, Turn
Row 2	*(Ch4, sl st in next st) from*rep across

Cut off a thread, leave a long tail for attaching purposes.

HALO

Rd 1	With **Bright Yellow+Gold metallic yarn:** Ch24, sl st in 1st ch to join in round [25]
Rd 2	sl st in each st around

Cut off a thread, leave a long tail for attaching purposes.

Angel

ARMS (make 2)
(work in continuous rounds)

Rd 1	**Wheat:** 5SC in magic ring [5] tighten the ring
Rd 2	INC in each st around [10]
Rd 3-5	SC in each st around [10]
	Change to Light Blue in last st. Cut off Wheat
Rd 6-7	**Light Blue:** SC in each st around [10]
Rd 8-17	SC in each st around [10]

Cut off a thread, leave a long tail for attaching purposes.

BOOTS (MAKE 2)
(work in continuous rounds)

Rd 1	**Light Blue:** 6SC in magic ring [6] tighten the ring
Rd 2	INC in each st around [12]
Rd 3	*(SC in next st, INC in next st)from*rep x6 [18]
Rd 4-5	SC in each st around [18]
Rd 6	*(SC in next st, SC2tog) from*rep x6 [12]
	Stuff a bit. Stitch edges together by SC in next 6 stitches inserting your hook through both layers and closing the opening.
	Cut off a thread leaving a long tail for sewing.

WINGS (make 2)
(work in rows)

White + White fur: Chain 14

| Row 1 | 2hdc in 3rd st from hook, Ch2, SC in next 11sts, Ch1, Turn |

| Row 2 | SC in next 10sts, Ch3, Turn |

| Row 3 | 2hdc in 3rd st from hook, Ch2, SC in next 10sts, Ch1, Turn |

| Row 4 | SC in next 9sts, Ch3, Turn |

| Row 5 | 2hdc in 3rd st from hook, Ch2, SC in next 9sts, Ch1, Turn |

| Row 6 | SC in next 8sts, Ch3, Turn |

| Row 7 | 2hdc in 3rd st from hook, Ch2, SC in next 8sts, |

Continue (corner): 2SC in same st as prev SC, SC in each of next 6 row

Cut off a thread leaving a long tail for attaching purposes.

ASSEMBLING

1. Sew the nose on the beard and then sew it on the body under the hat brim in front to 8 stitches FLO of Rd 1.

2. Sew the arms on the body under the hat brim in front to 4 stitches FLO of Rd 2 on both sides.

3. Hold the gnome upside down and sew the boots on the body to stitches FLO of Rd 23 on both sides.

4. Sew the hair on the body above the beard with nose and arms under the hat brim

Sew on the wings:
1) Start by pinning the wings on the back, following the illustration provided. Make sure the wing ends are visible from the front.
2) Using a tapestry needle and White thread, stitch the wings in multiple spots to secure them in place and prevent them from drooping. Ensure a tight fit against the back.
3) Repeat the same process to sew on the second wing, ensuring it is symmetrical to the first one.

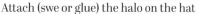

Attach (swe or glue) the halo on the hat

SIZE:
13cm/
5in

COLORS AND YARN

TOTAL FOR A PROJECT

Color		Yarn	Total for a project
Light Blue	⭐	Yarn Art Jeans 75	Approx. 20g/64meters
Wheat	⭐	Yarn Art Jeans 05	Approx. 5g/15meters
White	☆	Yarn Art Jeans 62	Approx. 15g/45meters
Bright Yellow	⭐	Yarn Art Jeans 35	Approx. 15g/48meters
Gold metallic yarn	⭐	DROPS Glitter	A little amount (optional)
White Fur**	☆	Rico Baby Teddy**	Approx. 10g/25meters (optional)

** You can use any fluffy yarn. I crocheted wings in double strand using one fluffy thread + one white thread of the main yarn. If your the fluffy thread is thick, you can crochet in a single strand

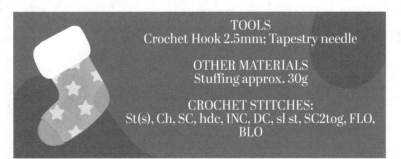

TOOLS
Crochet Hook 2.5mm; Tapestry needle

OTHER MATERIALS
Stuffing approx. 30g

CROCHET STITCHES:
St(s), Ch, SC, hdc, INC, DC, sl st, SC2tog, FLO, BLO

To effectively mark the beginning of each round, it is recommended to use a contrasting thread. This thread should be kept in place until your work is completed.

HAT

(work in continuous rounds)

Rd 1	**White:** 6SC in magic ring [6] tighten the ring
Rd 2	INC in each st around [12]
Rd 3	*(SC in next st, INC in next st)from*rep x6 [18]
Rd 4	*(SC in next st, INC in next st, SC in next st) from*rep x6 [24]
Rd 5	*(SC in next 3sts, INC in next st)from*rep x6 [30]
Rd 6	*(SC in next 2sts, INC in next st, SC in next 2sts) from*rep x6 [36]
Rd 7	SC in each st around[36]
Rd 8	*(SC in next 5sts, INC in next st)from*rep x6 [42]
Rd 9-11	SC in each st around [42]
Rd 12	*(SC in next 3sts, INC in next st, SC in next 3sts) from*rep x6 [48]
Rd 13-16	SC in each st around [48] Change to Light Blue in last stitch. Cut off White

CONTINUE - BODY

(WORK IN CONTINUOUS ROUNDS)

Note: We have numbered the rounds starting from 1 to make it easier for you to navigate

Rd 1	**Light Blue:** SC BLO in each st around [48]
Rd 2	SC in next 16sts, SC BLO in next 4sts (hair will be attached to theses sts), SC in next 2sts, SC BLO in next 4sts (a nose will be attached to theses sts), SC in next 2sts, SC in next 4 sts (hair will be attached to theses sts), SC in next 16 sts) [48]
Rd 3	SC in next 10sts, SC BLO in next 4sts (an arm will be attached to theses sts), SC in next 20sts, BLO in next 4sts (an arm will be attached to theses sts), SC in next 10sts) [48]
Rd 4-9	SC in each st around [48]
Rd 10	*(SC in next 5sts, INC in next st)from*rep x8 [56]
Rd 14-16	SC in each st around [56]
Rd 17	SC BLO in each st around [56] **Note:** the skirt will be crocheted on these stitches FLO later
Rd 18	*(SC in next 5sts, SC2tog) from*rep x8 [48]
Rd 19-20	SC in each st around [48]

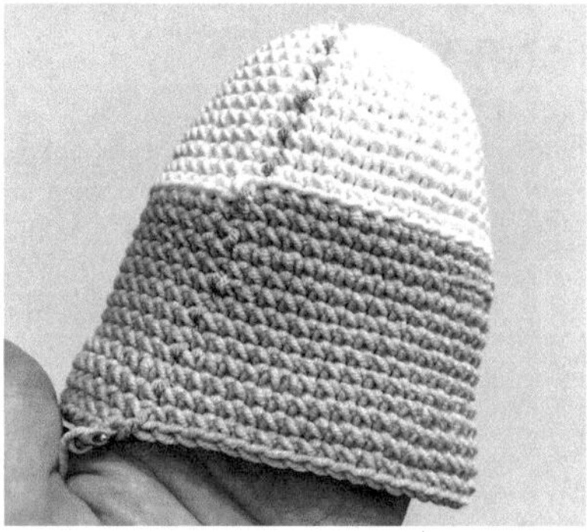

Rd 21	SC BLO in each st around [48]
Rd 22	*(SC in next 2sts, SC2tog, SC in next 2sts)from*rep x8 [40]
Rd 23	*(SC in next 3sts, SC2tog) from*rep x8 [32]
Rd 24	*(SC in next st, SC2tog, SC in next st)from*rep x8 [24]
Rd 25	*(SC in next st, SC2tog) from*rep x8 [16]
Rd 26	SC2tog x8 [8]

Cut off a thread, leave a long tail for sewing. Using this tail and a tapestry needle pull the tail through the last stitches FLO and tighten the opening. Weave in

SKIRT

Rd 1	Hold the body upside down and join **Light Blue**:to the first stitch FLO of Rd 16 of the body: Ch1, hdc FLO in each st around [57], sl st in 1st st of rd to join rd. Cut off a thread and weave in
Rd 2	Join **White:** Ch2, *(skip next st, work all [DC, Ch1, DC] in next st, skip next st, DC in next st) from*rep x14
Rd 3	*(4DC in 1Ch-space, skip next DC, SC in next DC) from*rep x14 [14 shells]

Cut off a thread and weave in

HAT BRIM

Rd 1	Hold the body upside down and work into stitches FLO of Rd 16 of the head with **White:** *(SC FLO in next 11sts, INC FLO in next st)from*rep x4 [52]
Rd 2	*(SC in next 6sts, INC in next st, SC in next 6sts)from*rep x4 [56]
Rd 3	*(SC in next 13sts, INC in next st)from*rep x4 [60]
Rd 4	*(hdc in next 5sts, 2hdc in next st)from*rep x10 [70]

Cut off a thread and weave in

Use the WINGS and BOOTS patterns from the project Angel on page 66. HALLO - page 65.
Use Wheat and NOSE pattern on page 110

ARMS make 2
(work in continuous rounds)

STEP 1. ARM

Rd 1	**Wheat:** 5SC in magic ring [5] tighten the ring
Rd 2	INC in each st around [10]
Rd 3-5	SC in each st around [10] Change to Light blue in last st. Cut off Wheat
Rd 6-7	**Light Blue:** SC in each st around [10]
Rd 8	SC BLO in each st around [10]
Rd 9-17	SC in each st around [10]

Cut off a thread leaving a long tail for attaching purposes.

STEP 2. CUFF

Rd 1	Join **White** and work into stitches FLO of Rd 7: SC FLO in each st around [10]
Rd 2	hdc in each st around [10] Cut off thread

Cut off a thread and weave in

HAIR (work in one piece) make 2

	Bright Yellow: Chain 29
HAIR 1	3hdc in 3nd st from hook, 3hdc in next 26sts;
HAIR 2	Chain 23, 3hdc in 3rd st from hook, 3hdc in next 20sts;
HAIR 3	Chain 19, 3hdc in 2nd st from hook, 3hdc in next 17sts

Cut off a thread leaving a long tail for attaching purpose.

ASSEMBLING

Sew the nose on the body under the hat brim in front to 4 stitches FLO of Rd 1 and hair to 4 stitches FLO on both side from the nose

Sew the arms on the body under the hat brim in front to 4 stitches FLO of Rd 2 on both sides.
Sew on the wings:
1) Start by pinning the wings onto the back, following the illustration provided. Make sure the wing ends are visible from the front.

2) Using a tapestry needle and White thread, stitch the wings in multiple spots to secure them in place and prevent them from drooping. Ensure a tight fit against the back.
3) Repeat the same process to sew on the second wing, ensuring it is symmetrical to the first one.
Sew the boots on the body to stitches FLO of Rd 20 on both sides.

Baby Angel

SIZE: 9cm/ 3.5in

COLORS AND YARN

Color		Yarn	Total for a project
Light Blue	★	Yarn Art Jeans 75	Approx. 12g/38meters
Wheat	☆	Yarn Art Jeans 05	Approx. 5g/15meters
White	☆	Yarn Art Jeans 62	Approx. 7g/20 meters
Bright Yellow	★	Yarn Art Jeans 35	Approx. 12g/38meters
Gold metallic yarn	★	DROPS Glitter	A little amount (optional)
White Fur**	☆	Rico Baby Teddy**	Approx. 10g/25meters (optional)

TOTAL FOR A PROJECT

** You can use any fluffy yarn. I crocheted wings in double strand using one fluffy thread + one white thread of the main yarn. If your the fluffy thread is thick, you can crochet in a single strand

TOOLS
Crochet Hook 2.5mm; Tapestry needle

OTHER MATERIALS
Stuffing approx. 15g

CROCHET STITCHES:
St(s), Ch, SC, hdc, INC, sl st, SC2tog, FLO, BLO

HEAD
(WORK IN CONTINUOUS ROUNDS)

Rd 1	**Bright Yellow:** 6SC in magic ring [6] tighten the ring
	Note: We will be working into the back loops only, while keeping the front loops accessible for creating the hair
Rd 2	INC BLO in each st around [12]
Rd 3	*(SC BLO in next st, INC BLO in next st)from*rep x6 [18]
Rd 4	*(SC BLO in next st, INC BLO in next st, SC BLO in next st) from*rep x6 [24]
Rd 5	*(SC BLO in next 3sts, INC BLO in next st)from*rep x6 [30]
Rd 6-9	SC BLO in each st around [30] Change to Light Blue in last stitch. Cut off Bright Yellow

CONTINUE - BODY
(WORK IN CONTINUOUS ROUNDS)

Note: We have numbered the rounds starting from 1 to make it easier for you to navigate when assembling

Rd 1-2	**Light Blue:** SC BLO in each st around [30]
Rd 3-4	SC in each st around [30]
Rd 5	*(SC in next 2sts, INC in next st, SC in next 2sts) from*rep x6 [36]
Rd 6-7	SC in each st around [36]
Rd 8	*(SC in next 4sts, INC in next st, SC in next 4sts) from*rep x4 [40]
Rd 9	SC in each st around [40]
Rd 10	*(SC in next 3sts, SC2tog) from*rep x8 [32]
Rd 11	SC in each st around [32]
	Stuff. Stuff as you work
Rd 12	SC BLO in each st around [32]

Rd 13	*(SC in next st, SC2tog, SC in next st)from*rep x8 [24]
Rd 14	*(SC in next st, SC2tog) from*rep x8 [16]
	Stuff
Rd 15	SC2tog x8 [8]

Cut off a thread, leave a long tail for sewing. Using this tail and a tapestry needle pull the tail through the last stitches FLO and tighten the opening. Weave in

HAIR
(work in continuous rounds)

| Rd 1-8 | Join **Bright Yellow** to any stitch of Rd 2 of the head and working into stitches FLO work: *(Ch2, sl st FLO in next st) from*rep around |

Cut off a thread and weave in

NOSE
(work in continuous rounds)

Rd 1	**Wheat:** 6SC in magic ring [6] tighten the ring
Rd 2	*(SC in next st, INC in next st)from*rep x3 [9]
Rd 3-4	SC in each st around [9]

Cut off a thread, leave a long tail for sewing. Using this tail and a tapestry needle pull the tail through the last stitches FLO and tighten the opening

HALO

| Rd 1 | With **Bright Yellow+Gold metalic yarn:** Ch24, sl st in 1st ch to join in round [25] |
| Rd 2 | sl st in each st around |

Cut off a thread, leave a long tail for attaching purposes.

ARMS (MAKE 2)

Wheat: Chain 10

| Row 1 | Make 2 unfinished hdc in 3rd st from hook, yarn over and pull through all loops on your hook, Ch2, sl st in same st as previous hdc, sl St in next 7sts |

Cut off a thread, leave a long tail for attaching purposes.

WINGS (make 2)
(work in rows)

White + White fur: Chain 12

Row 1 2hdc in 3rd st from hook, Ch2, SC in next 9sts, Ch1, Turn

Row 2 SC in next 8sts, Ch3, Turn

Row 3 2hdc in 3rd st from hook, Ch2, SC in next 8sts, Ch1, Turn

Row 4 SC in next 7sts, Ch3, Turn

Row 5 2hdc in 3rd st from hook, Ch2, SC in next 7sts, Ch1, Turn

Row 6 SC in next 6sts, Ch3, Turn

Row 7 2hdc in 3rd st from hook, Ch2, SC in next 6sts,

2SC in same st as prev SC, SC in each of next 6 Row

Cut off a thread, leave a long tail for attaching purposes.

BOOTS
(make 2) (work in rows)

Leave a long tail for sewing
Light Blue: Chain 12

Row 1	sl st in 2nd st from hook, sl st in next 10sts [11] Ch1, Turn
Row 2-3	sl st BLO in next 11sts [11] Ch1, Turn
Row 4	sl st BLO in next 9sts, [9] Ch1, Turn
Row 5-6	sl st BLO in next 7sts [7] Ch1, Turn
Row 7	sl st BLO in next 7 sts [7]

Cut off leaving a long tail approx. 10cm for sewing

LEG (make 1)

Wheat: Chain 30

Row 1	sl st in 2nd st from hook, sl st in each st across

Cut off a thread, leave a long tail for attaching purposes.

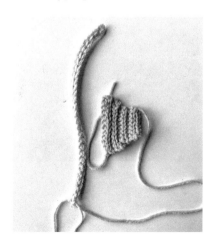

ASSEMBLING

Attach (sew or glue) the nose to stitches FLO of Rd 1 of the body

Insert the second end of the chain through the body and use your crochet hook to pull it out on the other side, where the second leg should be located.

Fold the boot in half as it's illustrated and sew along a back of the boot and front/top part, leaving the hole for inserting the leg

Insert on end of the chain (leg) into the boot and fix in plave (sew or glue).

And insert the end into the second boot and secure in place
Sew on the wings:
Sew the arms to the stitches FLO of Rd 2 of the body on both sides
Attach (sew or glue) the halo on the hat

Gnome Lumiere

**SIZE:
21 cm/
8.3 in**

COLORS AND YARN

TOTAL FOR A PROJECT

Color		Yarn	Total
Light Grey	⭐	Yarn Art Jeans 46	Approx. 25g/80meters
Light Green	⭐	Yarn Art Jeans 29	Approx. 7g/20 meters
Wheat	⭐	Yarn Art Jeans 05	Approx. 5g/15meters
Off-White	⭐	Yarn Art Jeans 03	Approx. 10g/30 meters
Bright Yellow	⭐	Yarn Art Jeans 35	Approx. 3g/10meters
Black (wick)	⭐	Yarn Art Jeans 53	A little amount
White	⭐	Yarn Art Jeans 62	Approx. 7g/25meters

To effectively mark the beginning of each round, it is recommended to use a contrasting thread. This thread should be kept in place until your work is completed.

CANDLE
(work in continuous rounds)

Rd 1	**Off White:** 7SC in magic ring [7] tighten the ring
Rd 2	INC in each st around [14]
Rd 3	*(SC in next st, INC in next st)from*rep x7 [21]
Rd 4	*(SC in next st, INC in next st, SC in next st)from*rep x7 [28]
Rd 5	*(SC in next 3sts, INC in next st)from*rep x7 [35]
Rd 6	BPsc in each st around [35]
Rd 7-21	SC in each st around [35] Change to Light Green in last st. Cut off Off-White

TOOLS
Crochet Hook 2.5mm; Tapestry needle

OTHER MATERIALS
Stuffing approx. 30g Optional: Red ribbon

CROCHET STITCHES:
St(s), Ch, SC, hdc, INC, sl st, SC2tog,
FLO, BLO, BPsc

Rd 22	**Light Green:** *(SC FLO in next 3sts, INC FLO in next st, SC FLO in next 3sts) from*rep x5 [40]

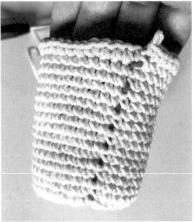

Rd 23	*(SC in next 2sts, INC in next st, SC in next 2sts) from*rep **x8** [48]
Rd 24	SC FLO in each st around [48]
Rd 25	*(SC in next 7sts, INC in next st)from*rep **x6** [54]
Rd 26	*(SC in next 4sts, INC in next st, SC in next 4ts) from*rep x6 [60]
Rd 27	*(SC in next 9sts, INC in next st)from*rep x6 [66]
Rd 28	SC in each st around [66]

Cut off Light Green and weave in

BODY (CANDELABRUM)
(WORK IN CONTINUOUS ROUNDS)

Rd 1	With **Light Grey** work BLO into stitches of Rd 23: SC BLO in each st around [48]

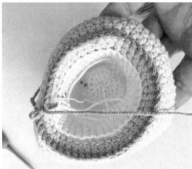

Rd 2	SC in next 20sts, SC BLO in next 8sts (we will attach a beard here), SC in next 20sts [48]
Rd 3	SC in next 10sts, SC BLO in next 4sts (the handle will be attached to these sts), SC in next 20sts, SC BLO in next 4sts (the handle will be attached to these sts), SC in next 10sts [48]

Rd 4- 7	SC in each st around [48]
Rd 8	*(SC in next 11sts, INC in next st)from*rep x4 [52]
Rd 9	SC in each st around [52]
Rd 10	*(SC in next 6sts, INC in next st, SC in next 6sts) from*rep x4 [56]
Rd 11	SC in each st around [56]
Rd 12	*(SC in next 13sts, INC in next st)from*rep x4 [60]
Rd 13	SC in each st around [60]
Rd 14	*(SC in next 7sts, INC in next st, SC in next 7sts) from*rep x4 [64]
Rd 15-17	SC in each st around [64]
Rd 18	*(SC in next 3sts, SC2tog, SC in next 3sts)from*rep x8 [56]
Rd 19-20	SC in each st around [56]
Rd 21	*(SC in next 5sts, SC2tog) from*rep x8 [48]

Stuff. Stuff as you work

Rd 22-23	SC in each st around [48]
Rd 24	SC BLO in each st around [48]

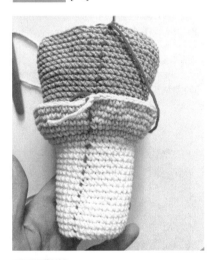

Rd 25	*(SC in next 2sts, SC2tog, SC in next 2sts) from*rep x8 [40]

Rd 26	*(SC in next 3sts, SC2tog) from*rep x8 [32]
Rd 27	*(SC in next st, SC2tog, SC in next st)from*rep x8 [24]
Rd 28	*(SC in next st, SC2tog) from*rep x8 [16]
	Stuff
Rd 29	SC2tog x8 [8]

Cut off a thread, leave a long tail for sewing. Using this tail and a tapestry needle sew pull the tail through the last stitches flo and tighten the opening.

Use Wheat and NOSE pattern on page 110
Use White and BEARD pattern #1 on page 110

DRIPS ON THE CANDLE

Rd 1	**Off White:** work in stitches of Rd 5 (see pic) of the candle: SC in each st around.

Rd 2 - DRIPS: sl st in next 2sts,
1) Ch10, 3hdc in 2nd st from hook, SC in next Ch, sl st in each Ch, sl st in next 3sts of Rd 1,
2) Ch6, 3hdc in 2nd st from hook, SC in next Ch, sl st in each Ch, sl st in next 4sts of Rd 1,
3) Ch9, 3hdc in 2nd st from hook, SC in next Ch, sl st in each Ch, sl st in next 5sts of Rd 1,
4) Ch6, 3hdc in 2nd st from hook, SC in next Ch, sl st in each Ch, sl st in next 6sts of Rd 1,
5) Ch5, 3hdc in 2nd st from hook, SC in next Ch, sl st in each Ch, sl st in next 3sts of Rd 1,
6) Ch10, 3hdc in 2nd st from hook, SC in next Ch, sl st in each Ch, sl st in next 6sts of Rd 1,
7) Ch8, 3hdc in 2nd st from hook, SC in next Ch, sl st in each Ch, sl st in next 6sts of Rd 1.
Cut off a thread and weave in.

HANDLES
(work in continuous rounds)

Rd 1	**Light Grey:** 6SC in magic ring [6] tighten the ring
Rd 2	*(SC in next st, INC in next st)from*rep x3 [9]
Rd 3-37	SC in each st around [9]

Cut off a thread, leave a long tail for attaching purposes

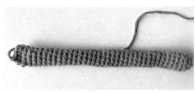

LIGHT
(work in continuous rounds)

Rd 1	**Bright Yellow:** 6SC in magic ring [6] tighten the ring
Rd 2	SC in each st around [6]
Rd 3	INC in each of next 2sts, SC in next 2sts, INC in next st, SC in next st [9]
Rd 4	SC in next st, INC in each of next 2sts, SC in next 5sts, INC in next st [12]
Rd 5-10	SC in each st around [12]
Rd 11	SC2tog x6 [6]

Cut off a thread leaving a long tail for attaching purposes.

ASSEMBLING

1. Attach (sew or glue) the drips on the candle.

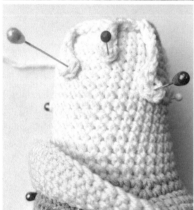

2. Embroider the wick on the light with Black and attach the light on top (sew or glue)

3. Sew the handles on the body.

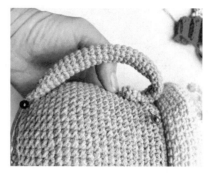

Sew the nose on the beard and attach the beard on the stitches FLO of Rd 1 of the body under the hat brim

A top end of the handle is attached to stitches FLO of Rd 2 of the body. Bend the handle and secure it in place on the hat brim.
A top end of the handle is attached to stitches FLO of Rd 23 of the body.

Optionally, tie a red ribbon on the candle.

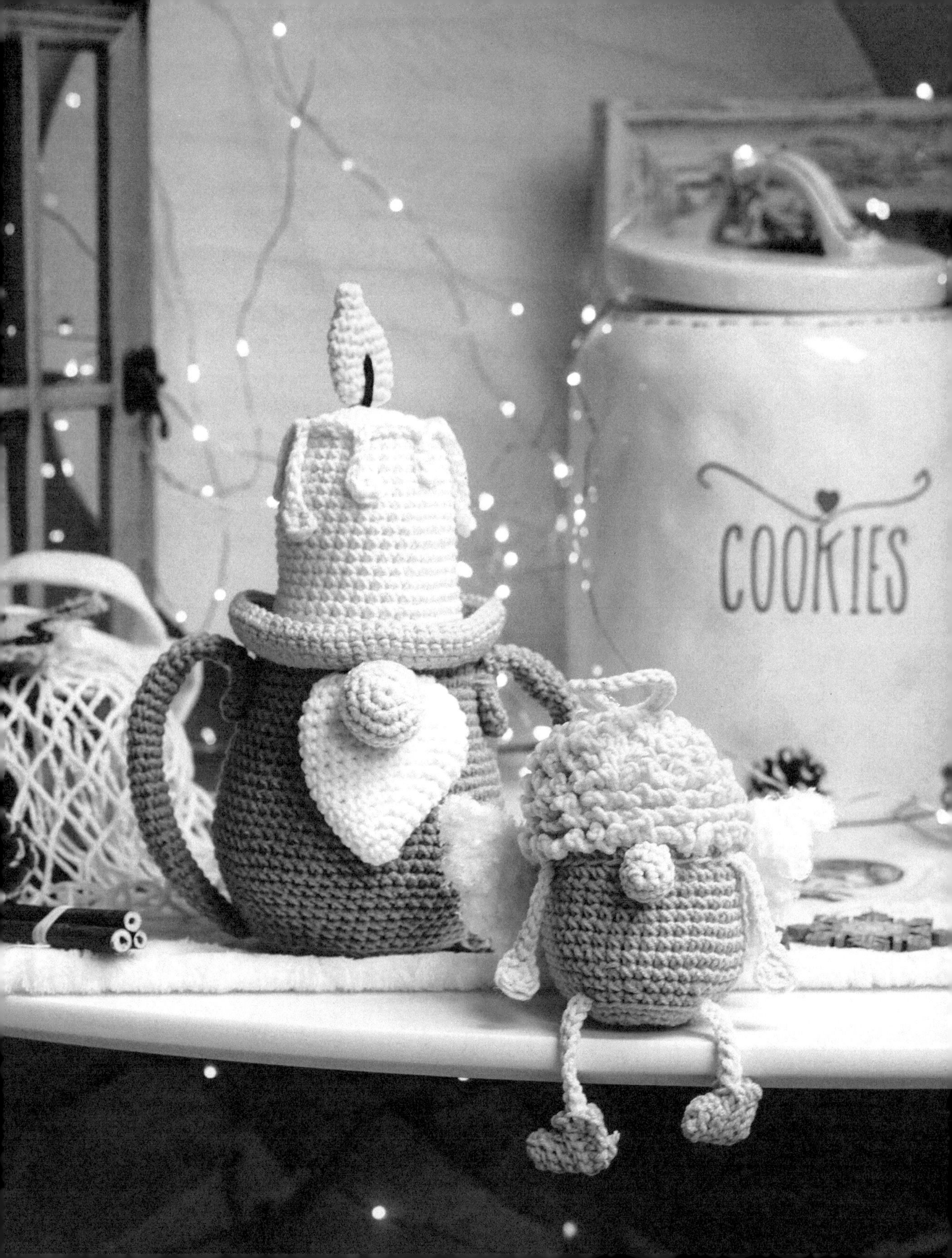
COOKIES

Snowmen

**SIZE:
17cm/
6.7in**

COLORS AND YARN			TOTAL FOR 1 GNOME
White		Yarn Art Jeans 62	Approx. 30g/96meters
Bright Orange		Yarn Art Jeans 77	Approx. 5g/17meters
Green/Grass Green		Yarn Art Jeans 29/ Yarn Art Jeans 69	Approx. 9g/28meters
Red/Blue		Yarn Art Jeans 90/ Yarn Art Jeans 76	Approx. 15g/48meters
Dark Brown		Yarn Art Jeans 70	Approx. 10g/35 meters

TOOLS
Crochet Hook 2.5mm; Tapestry needle

OTHER MATERIALS
Stuffing approx. 30g. Optional: 2 buttons

CROCHET STITCHES:
St(s), Ch, SC, hdc, INC, sl st, SC2tog,
FLO, BLO, hdc-whb

To effectively mark the beginning of each round, it is recommended to use a contrasting thread. This thread should be kept in place until your work is completed.

STEP 1. BODY
(work in continuous rounds)

Rd 1	**White:** 6SC in magic ring [6] tighten the ring
Rd 2	INC in each st around [12]
Rd 3	*(SC in next st, INC in next st)from*rep x6 [18]
Rd 4	*(SC in next st, INC in next st, SC in next st) from*rep x6 [24]
Rd 5	*(SC in next 3sts, INC in next st)from*rep x6 [30]
Rd 6	*(SC in next 2sts, INC in next st, SC in next 2sts) from*rep x6 [36]
Rd 7	*(SC in next 5sts, INC in next st)from*rep x6 [42]
Rd 8	*(SC in next 3sts, INC in next st, SC in next 3sts) from*rep x6 [48]
Rd 9-18	SC in each st around [48]
Rd 19	SC in next 22sts, SC BLO in next 4 sts(a nose will be attached to these sts), SC in next 22sts [48]
Rd 20-27	SC in each st around [48]
Rd 28	SC in next 13sts, SC BLO in next 3 sts (an arm will be attached to these sts), SC in next 20sts, SC BLO in next 3sts, SC in next 9sts (an arm will be attached to these sts) [48]
Rd 29-30	SC in each st around [48]

Rd 31	*(SC in next 7sts, INC in next st)from*rep x6 [54]
Rd 32-33	SC in each st around [54]
Rd 34	*(SC in next 4sts, INC in next st, SC in next 4sts) from*rep x6 [60]
Rd 35-36	SC in each st around [60]
Rd 37	*(SC in next 9sts, INC in next st)from*rep x6 [66]
Rd 38-41	SC in each st around [66]
Rd 42	*(SC in next 9sts, SC2tog) from*rep x6 [60]
Rd 43	SC in each st around [60]
	Stuff. Stuff as you work
Rd 44	*(SC in next 4sts, SC2tog, SC in next 4sts)from*rep x6 [54]
Rd 45	SC in each st around [54]
Rd 46	*(SC in next 7sts, SC2tog) from*rep x6 [48]
Rd 47	SC in each st around [48]
Rd 48	SC BLO in each st around [48] Note: we will crochet a stand into these stitches FLO later
Rd 49	*(SC in next 2sts, SC2tog, SC in next 2sts)from*rep x8 [40]
Rd 50	*(SC in next 3sts, SC2tog) from*rep x8 [32]
Rd 51	*(SC in next st, SC2tog, SC in next st)from*rep x6 [24]
Rd 52	*(SC in next st, SC2tog) from*rep x8 [16] Stuff well
Rd 53	SC2tog x8 [8]

Cut off a thread, leave a long tail for sewing. Using this tail and a tapestry needle pull the tail through the last stitches FLO and tighten the opening. Weave in

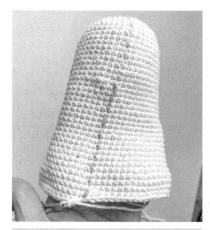

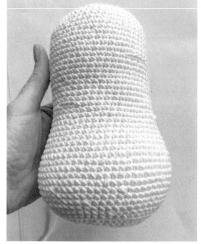

STEP 2. STAND

Hold the body upside down and with **White** work into stitches FLO of Rd Rd 47 of the body(start from any stitch):
Ch1, SC FLO in each st around [48]
Cut off a thread and weave in

NOSE

(work in continuous rounds)

Rd 1	**Bright Orange:** 6SC in magic ring [6] tighten the ring
Rd 2	INC in each st around [12]
Rd 3	*(SC in next st, INC in next st)from*rep x6 [18]
Rd 4-5	SC in each st around [18]
Rd 6	*(SC in next st, SC2tog) from*rep x6 [12]

Cut off a thread leaving a long tail for attaching purposes. Stuff the nose with a small amount of stuffing

MITTENS+ARMS

(there is the pattern for the sticks on the next page)

STEP 1. MITTENS (work in continuous rounds)

Rd 1	**Red:** 6SC in magic ring [6] tighten the ring
Rd 2	INC in each st around [12]
Rd 3-5	SC in each st around [12]
Rd 6	*(SC in next st, SC2tog)from*rep x4 [8] Change to Dark Brown in last st. Cut off Red. Stuff a bit
Rd 7	**Dark Brown:** SC BLO in each st around [8]
Rd 8-18	SC in each st around. [8] Cut off thread leaving a long tail for attaching purposes.

STEP 2. CUFF

	Red: Chain 11
Row 1	hdc in 2nd st from hook, hdc in next 9sts [10]

Attach the cuff to the arm

STEP 3. THUMB

Red: Embroider a thumb with several stitches

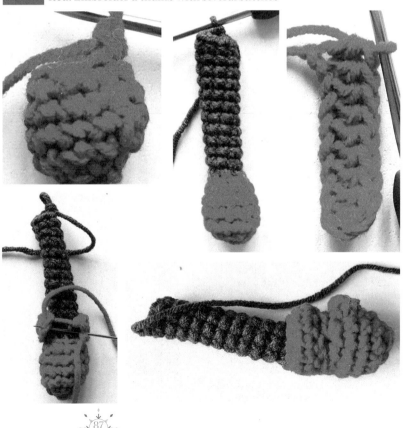

STICKS
(work in continuous rounds)

STEP 1. LONG STICK

Rd 1	**Dark Brown:** 6SC in magic ring [6] tighten the ring
Rd 2-5	SC in each st around [6]
Rd 6	SC in each st to last st, sl st [6] Cut off a thread

STEP 2. SHORT STICK

Rd 1	**Dark Brown:** 6SC in magic ring [6] tighten the ring
Rd 2-3	SC in each st around [6] Do not cut off thread and go to the next step

STEP 3. ASSEMBLE

Arrange together the long and the short sticks as illustrated in mage below

Insert your hook through stitches of both fabrics and make SC Make SC in next 3 stitches

the same way

Continue crocheting SC in next 3 stitches of the

stick that is on top and then continue working SC in next 6 stitches of the edge, make 10 rounds

SCARF (work in rows)

Green/Grass Green: Chain 6

Row 1	SC in 2nd st from hook, SC in next 4sts [5] Ch1, Turn
Row 20-30	SC BLO in each st across [5] Ch1, Turn.

Fold in half and stitch short edges together by SC on a wrong side.
Cut off a thread and weave in

HAT (work in rows)

Red/Blue: Chain 24

Row 1	hdc in 2nd st from hook, hdc in next 19 sts, SC in next 3sts [23] Ch1, Turn
Row 2	SC FLO in next 3 sts, hdc-whb in next 20 sts (scan QR code to watch the video tutorial) [23] Ch1, Turn

Scan to watch a video tutorial "hdc-whb"

| Row 3 | hdc BLO in next 20 sts, SC BLO in next 3sts [23] Ch1, Turn |
| Row 4-35 | Repeat pattern for Row 2-3 |

Fold in half and stitch short edges together by SC on a wrong side. On the side with SCs, gather the edge on a thread and pull it off.
Sew on a pompom or crochet a ball like other gnomes.
Cut off thread and weave in

Make a fluffy pom-pon using White forte red hat or Red for the blue hat. You can also crochet the pompon using the pompon pattern on page 111

ASSEMBLING

Sew the nose to stitches FLO of Rd 18 in front of the body.
Sew the arms/sticks on the body to stitches FLO of Rd 27 on both sides. Sew or glue buttons on the body in front.
Put on the hat and scarf.

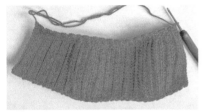

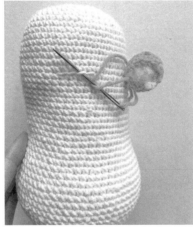

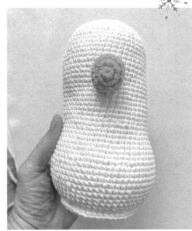

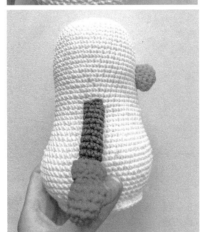

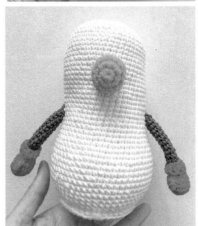

Christmas Cup

SIZE: 30cm/ 12in

COLORS AND YARN			TOTAL FOR A PROJECT
Fog Grey		Yarn Art Jeans 49	Approx. 15g/48meters
White		Yarn Art Jeans 62	Approx. 15g/48meters
Wheat		Yarn Art Jeans 05	Approx. 6g/19meters
Red		Yarn Art Jeans 90	Approx. 25g/80meters
Black		Yarn Art Jeans 53	Approx. 5g15meters
Light Green		Yarn Art Jeans 29	Approx. 5g/15meters

TOOLS
Crochet Hook 2.5mm; Tapestry needle

OTHER MATERIALS
Stuffing approx. 50g

CROCHET STITCHES:
St(s), Ch, SC, DC, hdc, INC, sl st,
SC2tog, FLO, BLO

To effectively mark the beginning of each round, it is recommended to use a contrasting thread. This thread should be kept in place until your work is completed.

STEP 1. CUP
(work in continuous rounds)

Rd 1	**Red:** 8SC in magic ring [8] tighten the ring
Rd 2	INC in each st around [16]
Rd 3	*(SC in next st, INC in next st)from*rep x8 [24]
Rd 4	*(SC in next st, INC in next st, SC in next st)from*rep x8 [32]
Rd 5	*(SC in next 3sts, INC in next st)from*rep x8 [40]
Rd 6	*(SC in next 2sts, INC in next st, SC in next 2sts)from*rep x8 [48]
Rd 7	*(SC in next 5sts, INC in next st)from*rep x8 [56]
Rd 8	*(SC in next 3sts, INC in next st, SC in next 3sts)from*rep x8 [64]

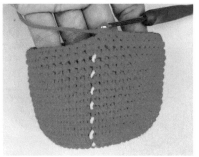

Rd 9-21	SC in each st around [64]
Rd 22	SC FLO in each st around [64]

Rd 23	SC in each st around [64] Change to Black in last st. Cut off Red
Rd 24	**Black:** SC in each st around [64]
Rd 25	hdc in each st around [64]

Cut off a thread and weave in

STEP 2. BODY
(work in continuous rounds)

Rd 1	Hold the cup upside down and work into the stitches BLO of Rd 21 of the cup with **Fog Grey:** SC BLO in each st around [64]

Rd 2	SC in each st around [64]
Rd 3	*(SC in next 3sts, SC2tog, SC in next 3sts)from*rep x8 [56]
Rd 4-5	SC in each st around [56]
Rd 6	*(SC in next 5sts, SC2tog) from*rep x8 [48]
Rd 7-9	SC in each st around [48]
Rd 10	SC in next 10sts, SC BLO in next 4sts (an arm will be attached to these sts), SC in next 20sts, SC BLO in next 4sts (an arm will be attached to these sts), SC in next 10sts [48]
Rd 11-12	SC in each st around [48]
Rd 13	SC in next 20sts, SC BLO in next 8sts (a beard will be attached to these sts), SC in next 20sts [48] Change to Red in last st. Cut off Fog grey

Rd 14	From this round we work a hat. **Red:** SC BLO in each st around [48] Note: we will crochet the hat brim in these stitches FLO later
Rd 15	*(SC in next 7sts, SC2tog, SC in next 7sts)from*rep x3 [45] Change to White in last st. Leave Red on WS

Rd 16-17	**White:** SC in each st around [45] Change to Red in last st. Leave White on WS
Rd 18	**Red:** *(SC in next 13sts, SC2tog)from*rep x3 [42]
Rd 19	SC in each st around [42] Change to White in last st. Leave Red on WS
Rd 20	**White:** SC in each st around [42]

Stuff. Stuff as you work

Rd 21	*(SC in next 6sts, SC2tog, SC in next 6sts)from*rep x3 [39] Change to Red in last st. Leave White on WS
Rd 22-23	**Red:** SC in each st around [39] Change to White in last st. Leave Red on WS
Rd 24	**White:** *(SC in next 11sts, SC2tog)from*rep x3[36]

Rd 25	SC in each st around [36] Change to Red in last st. Leave White on WS
Rd 26	**Red:** SC in each st around [36]
Rd 27	*(SC in next 5sts, SC2tog, SC in next 5sts)from*rep x3 [33] Change to White in last st. Leave Red on WS
Rd 28-29	**White:** SC in each st around [33] Change to Red in last st. Leave White on WS
Rd 30	**Red:** *(SC in next 9sts, SC2tog)from*rep x3[30]
Rd 31	SC in each st around [30] Change to White in last st. Leave Red on WS
Rd 32	**White:** SC in each st around [30]
Rd 33	*(SC in next 4sts, SC2tog, SC in next 4sts)from*rep x3 [27] Change to Red in last st. Leave White on WS
Rd 34-35	**Red:** SC in each st around [27] Change to White in last st. Leave Red on WS
Rd 36	**White:** *(SC in next 7sts, SC2tog)from*rep x3[24]
Rd 37	SC in each st around [24] Change to Red in last st. Leave White on WS
Rd 38	**Red:** SC in each st around [24]
Rd 39	*(SC in next 3sts, SC2tog, SC in next 3sts)from*rep x3[21] Change to White in last st. Leave Red on WS

Stuff. Stuff as you work

Rd 40-41	**White:** SC in each st around [21] Change to Red in last st. Leave White on WS
Rd 42	**Red:** *(SC in next 5sts, SC2tog)from*rep x3[18]
Rd 43	SC in each st around [18] Change to White in last st. Leave Red on WS
Rd 44	**White:** *(SC in next 2sts, SC2tog, SC in next 2sts)from*rep x3 [15]
Rd 45	SC in each st around [15] Change to Red in last st. Cuf off White

Rd 46-47	**Red:** SC in each st around [15]
Rd 48	*(SC in next 3sts, SC2tog) from*rep x3[12]
Rd 49-50	SC in each st around [12]
Rd 51	*(SC in next st, SC2tog, SC in next st)from*rep x3[9]
Rd 52-53	SC in each st around [9]
Rd 54	*(SC in next st, SC2tog) from*rep x3[6]
Rd 55-56	SC in each st around [6]

Cut off a thread and weave in

STEP 3. HAT BRIM

Rd 1	Hold the body upside down. Start from the beg of Rd 13 - Body. Join **Red** and work into stitches FLO: *(SC FLO in next 5sts, INC FLO in next st)from*rep x8 [56]

Rd 2	*(SC in next 3sts, INC in next st, SC in next 3sts)from*rep x8 [64] Change to White in last st. Leave Red on WS
Rd 3	**White:** *(SC in next 7sts, INC in next st)from*rep x8 [72]
Rd 4	*(SC in next 4sts, INC in next st, SC in next 4sts)from*rep x8 [80] Change to Red in last st. Cut off White
Rd 5	**Red:** *(SC in next 9sts, INC in next st)from*rep x8 [88]
Rd 6	SC in each st around [88]
Rd 7	Sl st in in each st around [88]

Cut off a thread and weave in

	Bow: Light green. Crochet a chain. The chain should be long enough to create a charming bow on a gnome's hat.

Use Wheat and NOSE pattern on page 110
Use Light Green and POMPON pattern on page 111

CUP HANDLE
(WORK IN CONTINUOUS ROUNDS)

Rd 1	**Red:** 6SC in magic ring [6] tighten the ring
Rd 2	*(SC in next st, INC in next st)from*rep x3 [9]
Rd 3-16	Stuff as you work SC in each st around [9]

Cut off a thread leaving a long tail for attaching purposes..

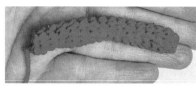

ARMS (make 2)
(work in continuous rounds)

Rd 1	**Wheat:** 5SC in magic ring [5] tighten the ring
Rd 2	INC in each st around [10]
Rd 3-5	SC in each st around [10] Change to Fog Grey in last st. Cut off Wheat
Rd 6-15	**Fog Grey:** SC in each st around

Cut off a thread leaving a long tail for attaching purposes.

BEARD

The beard consists of 3 parts. We are going to crochet each part separately and then join them together.

STEP 1. PART #1

Rd 1	**White:** 6SC in magic ring [6] tighten the ring
Rd 2	INC in each st around [12]
Rd 3-4	SC in each st around [12]
Rd 5	SC in each st around [12], sl st in next st

Cut off a thread

STEP 2. PARTS #3,2

Rd 1	**White:** 6SC in magic ring [6] tighten the ring
Rd 2	INC in each st around [12]
Rd 3	SC in each st around [12]
Rd 4	For the third part: SC in next 11sts, sl st in next st. Cut off a thread.

For the second part: SC in each st around. Do not cut off a thread, proceed to STEP 3: Assembling

STEP 3. ASSEMBLE
Find a photo tutorial on page 111.

Rd 1	Arrange all parts 2-1-3 as illustrated in the image below and join them working in edge stitches: SC in next 6sts of the part#2 SC in next 6sts of the part#1, SC in next 12sts of the part#3, SC in next 6sts of the part #1, SC in next 6sts of the part #2 [36]
Rd 2	SC in next 5sts, SC2tog, SC in next 4sts, SC2tog, SC in next 10sts, SC2tog,SC in next 4sts,SC2tog, SC in next 5sts [32]
Row 3	*(SC2tog, SC in next 3sts, SC2tog, SC in next 2sts, SC2tog, SC in next 3sts, SC2tog)from*rep x2 [24]

ASSEMBLING

Sew the nose and the beard together

Sew the arms on the body under the hat brim in front to 4 stitches FLO of Rd 9 of the body on both sides.

Sew the cup handle onto the cup, aligning it vertically with the arm.

Sew the beard with nose on the body under the hat brim in front to 8 stitches FLO of Rd 12 of the body.

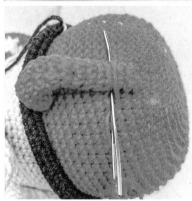

Sew or glue the pompom on the hat
Embroider snowflakes with White

Christmas Elf

SIZE:
30 cm/6.3in
(excl. legs
and hat)

COLORS AND YARN			TOTAL FOR A PROJECT
White	☆	Yarn Art Jeans 62	Approx. 15g/48meters
Wheat	☆	Yarn Art Jeans 05	Approx. 10g/32meters
Red	★	Yarn Art Jeans 90	Approx. 20g/65meters
Grass Green	★	Yarn Art Jeans 69	Approx. 30g/96meters
Brown	★	Yarn Art Jeans 40	Approx. 7g/22meters

TOOLS
Crochet Hook 2.5mm. Tapestry needle

OTHER MATERIALS
Stuffing approx. 50g
Decorative buttons x2

CROCHET STITCHES:
St(s), Ch, SC, DC, hdc, INC, sl st,
SC2tog, FLO, BLO

To effectively mark the beginning of each round, it is recommended to use a contrasting thread. This thread should be kept in place until your work is completed.

STEP 1. SUPPLEMENTARY PART
(we will use it to separate a hat)
(work in continuous rounds)

Rd 1	**Wheat:** 6SC in magic ring [6] tighten the ring
Rd 2	INC in each st around [12]
Rd 3	*(SC in next st, INC in next st) from*rep x6 [18]
Rd 4	*(SC in next st, INC in next st, SC in next st)from*rep x6 [24]
Rd 5	*(SC in next 3sts, INC in next st)from*rep x6 [30]
Rd 6	*(SC in next 2sts, INC in next st, SC in next 2sts)from*rep x6 [36]
Rd 7	*(SC in next 5sts, INC in next st)from*rep x6 [42]

Cut off a thread and weave in

STEP 2. BODY

Rd 1	**Grass Green:** 8SC in magic ring [8] tighten the ring
Rd 2	INC in each st around [16]
Rd 3	*(SC in next st, INC in next st)from*rep x8 [24]
Rd 4	*(SC in next st, INC in next st, SC in next st) from*rep x8 [32]

Rd 5	*(SC in next 3sts, INC in next st)from*rep x8 [40]
Rd 6	*(SC in next 2sts, INC in next st, SC in next 2sts) from*rep x8 [48]
Rd 7	*(SC in next 5sts, INC in next st)from*rep x8 [56]
Rd 8	*(SC in next 3sts, INC in next st, SC in next 3sts) from*rep x8 [64]
Rd 9	SC in next 14sts, SC BLO in next 10sts a leg will be attached to these sts), SC in next 6sts, SC BLO in next 10sts (a leg will be attached to these sts), SC in next 24sts [64]
Rd 10-17	SC in each st around [64] Change to Red in last st. Cut off Grass Green **Note:** into stitches of Rd 17 we will work a belt

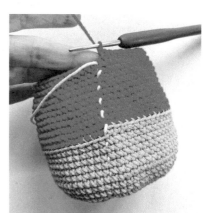

Rd 18	**Red:** SC BLO in each st around [64]
Rd 19-20	SC in each st around [64]
Rd 21	*(SC in next 3sts, SC2tog, SC in next 3sts)from*rep x8 [56]
Rd 22-24	SC in each st around [56]

Rd 25	*(SC in next 5sts, SC2tog) from*rep x8 [48]
Rd 26-27	SC in each st around [48]
Rd 28	SC in next 10sts, SC BLO in next 4sts (an arm will be attached to these sts), SC in next 20sts, SC BLO in next 4sts (an arm will be attached to these sts), SC in next 10sts [48]
Rd 29	SC in each st around [48]
Rd 30	SC BLO in each st around [48] **Note:** the collar will be crocheted to these stitches FLO later
Rd 31	SC in next 20 sts, SC BLO in next 8sts (a beard with nose will be attached to these sts), SC in next 20sts [48]

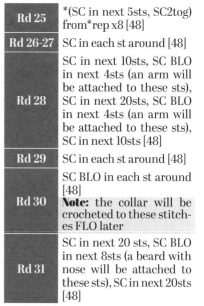

STEP 3. HAT

Rd 32	SC BLO in each st around [48] **Note:** a hat brim will be crocheted on these sts FLO
Rd 33	*(SC in next 7sts, SC2tog, SC in next 7sts)from*rep x3 [45] Change to White in last st. Do not cut off Red, leave it on the WS

Leave a non-working thread on WS and cut off a thread when it's stated in the pattern

Rd 34-35	**White:** SC in each st around [45] Change to Red in last st.
Rd 36	**Red:** *(SC in next 13sts, SC2tog)from*rep x3 [42]
Rd 37	Stuff the body. Grad the supplementary part made in Step 1 and put it inside of the opening. This round we should work through both edges: SC in each st around [42] Change to White in last st. Leave Red on WS

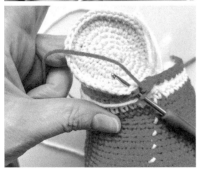

Rd 38	**White:** SC in each st around [42]
Rd 39	*(SC in next 6sts, SC2tog, SC in next 6sts)from*rep x3 [39] Change to Red in last st. Leave White on WS
Rd 40-41	**Red:** SC in each st around [39]] Change to White in last st

Rd 42	*(SC in next 11sts, SC-2tog)from*rep x3[36]
Rd 43	SC in each st around [36] Change to Red in last st.
Rd 44	**Red:** SC in each st around [36]
Rd 45	*(SC in next 5sts, SC2tog, SC in next 5sts)from*rep x3 [33] Change to White in last st.
Rd 46-47	**White:** SC in each st around [33] Change to Red in last st.
Rd 48	**Red:** *(SC in next 9sts, SC2tog)from*rep x3 [30]
Rd 49	SC in each st around [30]

Now we are going to move the beginning of the round to make a seam on the back of the hat. To make it work SC in next 5sts, Change to White in last st and place a marker of beginning of the round here.

Rd 50	**White:** SC in each st around [30]

Rd 51	*(SC in next 4sts, SC2tog, SC in next 4sts)from*rep x3 [27] Change to Red in last st.
Rd 52-53	**Red:** SC in each st around [27] Change to White in last st.
Rd 54	**White:** *(SC in next 7sts, SC2tog)from*rep x3 [24]
Rd 55	SC in each st around [24] Change to Red in last st.
Rd 56	**Red:** SC in each st around [24]

Rd 57	*(SC in next 3sts, SC2tog, SC in next 3sts)from*rep x3 [21] Change to White in last st.
Rd 58-59	**White:** SC in each st around [21] Change to Red in last st.
Rd 60	*(SC in next 5sts, SC2tog) from*rep x3 [18]
Rd 61	SC in each st around [18] Change to White in last st.
Rd 62	**White:** *(SC in next 2sts, SC2tog, SC in next 2sts) from*rep x3 [15]
Rd 63	SC in each st around [15] Change to Red in last st.
Rd 64-65	**Red:** SC in each st around [15] Change to White in last st.
Rd 66	**White:** *(SC in next 3sts, SC2tog)from*rep x3 [12]
Rd 67	SC in each st around [12] Change to Red in last st. Cut off White
Rd 68	**Red:** SC in each st around [12]
Rd 69	*(SC in next st, SC2tog, SC in next st)from*rep x3 [9]
Rd 70-71	SC in each st around [9]
Rd 72	*(SC in next st, SC2tog) from*rep x3 [6]
Rd 73-74	SC in each st around [6]

Cut off a thread, leave a long tail for sewing. Using this tail and a tapestry needle pull the tail through the last stitches FLO and tighten the opening. Weave in

STEP 4. COLLAR

Rd 1	Hold the gnome upside down. Start from the beginning of Rd 29 and work into the stitches FLO with **White:** *(Ch3, sl st in 2nd st from hook, hdc in next Ch, skip next 2sts of the main detail, SC FLO in next st)from*rep around [16 shells]

Cut off a thread and weave in

STEP 5. HAT BRIM

Rd 1	Start from the beginning of Rd 31 and work into the stitches FLO with 31 **Grass Green:** *(SC FLO in next 7sts, INC FLO in next st)from*rep x6 [54]
Rd 2-3	SC in each st around [54]
Rd 4	*(skip next 2sts, work al in next stitch [3DC, Ch3, sl st in Top of prev DC, 3DC], skip next 2sts, SC in next st) from*rep x9 [9 shells]

Cut off a thread and weave in

STEP 6. BELT

Rd 1 Start from the last st of Rd 17 and work into the stitches FLO with **Grass Green**: SC FLO in each st around [64]

Cut off a thread and weave in

Use Wheat and NOSE pattern on page 110
Use Brown and BEARD pattern #1 on page 110
Use Grass Green and the pompon pattern on page 111

ARMS
(work in continuous rounds)
STEP 1. ARMS

Rd 1 **Wheat:** 5SC in magic ring [5] tighten the ring

Rd 2	INC in each st around [10]
Rd 3-5	SC in each st around [10] Change to Red in last st. Cut off Wheat
Rd 6-7	**Red:** SC in each st around
Rd 8	SC BLO in each st around
Rd 9-15	SC in each st around

Cut off a thread leaving a long tail for attaching purposes

STEP 2. CUFF
(work in continuous rounds)

Rd 1	Hold the arm upside down and with **White** work into stitches FLO of Rd 7: SC FLO in each st around [10]
Rd 2	SC in each st around [10]
Rd 3	*(Ch1, sl st in next st) from*rep around

Cut off a thread and weave in

STRAPS
(make 2)

Grass Green: Chain 30 [30]

Row 1 sl st in 2nd st from hook, sl st in each st across [29]

Cut off a thread leaving a long tail for attaching purposes

LEG
(work in continuous rounds)
STEP 1. LEG

Rd 1	**White**: 6SC in magic ring [6] tighten the ring
Rd 2	*(SC in next st, INC in next st)from*rep x3 [9]
Rd 3-40	SC in each st around [9] Change to Grass Green in last st. Cut off White
Rd 41-42	**Grass Green:** SC in each st around [9]
Rd 43	SC BLO in each st around [9]
Rd 44	SC in each st around [9]

Cut off a thread leaving a long tail for sewing. Twist Red around the leg and weave in ends

STEP 2. CUFF
(work in continuous rounds)

Rd 1 Work in stitches FLO of Rd 42 of the leg with **Grass Green:** hdc FLO in each st around [9]

Rd 2	hdc in each st around [9], sl st in next st (extra st)

Cut off a thread and weave in. This side of the leg will be attached to the boot.

STEP 3. PANTS
(work in continuous rounds)

	Chain 19, sl st in 1st ch to join in round [20]
Rd 1-3	SC each st around [20]
Rd 4	(SC in next 3sts, INC in next st)from*rep x5 [25]
Rd 5	(SC in next 2sts, INC in next st, SC in next 2sts)from*rep x5 [25]
Rd 6	SC in each st around [30]

Rd 7	(SC in next st, SC-2tog) from*rep x10 [20]
Rd 8	SC2tog x10 [10]
Rd 9	SC in each st around [10]

Cut off a thread leaving a long tail for sewing. Insert the leg into the pants through the wide opening and securely fix it in place using a tapestry needle.

BOOTS
(work in continuous rounds)

Rd 1	**Grass Green:** 4SC in magic ring [4] tighten the ring
Rd 2	(SC in next st, INC in next st) from*rep x2 [6]
Rd 3	INC in next 2sts, SC in next 4 sts [8]
Rd 4	SC in next st, INC in next 2sts, SC in next 5 sts [10]
Rd 5	SC in next 2sts, INC in next 2sts, SC in next 6sts [12]
Rd 6-8	SC in each st around [12]
Row 9	Now work in rows: SC in next 5 sts [5] Ch1, Turn
Row 10-11	SC in next 9sts [9] Ch1, Turn

To create a back seam, stitch the edges of the boot on the wrong side. Once stitched, proceed to stuff the boot. Remember to leave the opening on the top of the boot for attaching the leg. Insert the leg into the opening and secure in place.

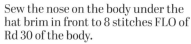

EARS (make 2)

(work in continuous rounds)

Rd 1	**Wheat:** 4SC in magic ring [4] tighten the ring
Rd 2	*(SC in next st, INC in next st)from*rep x2 [6]
Rd 3	*(SC in next st, INC in next st)from*rep x3 [9]
Rd 4	*(SC in next st, INC in next st, SC in next st)from*rep x3 [12]
Rd 5-7	SC in each st around [12]
Rd 8	SC2tog x6 [6]

Cut off a thread, leave a long tail for sewing. Using this tail and a tapestry needle pull the tail through the last stitches FLO, stuff and tighten the opening. Leave the tail for attaching purposes

ASSEMBLING

Attach (sew or glue) the nose on the beard.

Sew the nose on the body under the hat brim in front to 8 stitches FLO of Rd 30 of the body.

Sew the arms on the body under the hat brim in front to 4 stitches FLO of Rd 27 on both sides.

Sew the straps on the body
Hold the body upside down and sew the pants with legs on the body to 10 stitches FLO of Rd 8 on both sides.

Sew the ears on the body right above the arms on both sides.

Christmas Tree

**SIZE:
30 cm/
12 in**

COLORS AND YARN

TOTAL FOR A PROJECT

Color		Yarn	Total
Honey caramel		Yarn Art Jeans 07	Approx. 15g/48meters
White		Yarn Art Jeans 62	Approx. 10g/35meters
Wheat		Yarn Art Jeans 05	Approx. 5g/16meters
Bright Green		Yarn Art Jeans 52	Approx. 25g/80meters
Red		Yarn Art Jeans 90	Approx. 10g/35meters

TOOLS
Crochet Hook 2.5mm; Tapestry needle;
Stitch markers

OTHER MATERIALS
Stuffing approx. 50g

CROCHET STITCHES:
St(s), Ch, SC, DC, hdc, INC,
sl st, SC2tog, FLO, BLO

To effectively mark the beginning of each round, it is recommended to use a contrasting thread. This thread should be kept in place until your work is completed.

STEP 1. HAT + BODY
(work in continuous rounds)

Rd 1	**Bright Green:** 6SC in magic ring [6] tighten the ring
Rd 2	SC in each st around [6]
Rd 3	*(INC in next st, SC in next st)from*rep x3[9]
Rd 4	SC in each st around [9]
Rd 5	*(SC in next st, INC in next st, SC in next st) from*rep x3 [12]
Rd 6-7	SC in each st around [12]
Rd 8	*(SC in next 3sts, INC in next st)from*rep x3 [15]
Rd 9-11	SC in each st around [15]
Rd 12	*(SC in next 2sts, INC in next st, SC in next 2sts) from*rep x3 [18]
Rd 13-14	SC in each st around [18]
Rd 15	*(SC in next 5sts, INC in next st)from*rep x3 [21]
Rd 16-17	SC in each st around [21]
Rd 18	*(SC in next 3sts, INC in next st, SC in next 3sts) from*rep x3 [24]
Rd 19	SC in each st around [24]
Rd 20	SC BLO in each st around [24] Note: we will work Ruffles #1 into these stitches FLO
Rd 21	*(SC in next 7sts, INC in next st)from*rep x3 [27]
Rd 22-23	SC each st around [27]
Rd 24	*(SC in next 4sts, INC in next st, SC in next 4sts) from*rep x3 [30]
Rd 25	SC in each st around [30]
Rd 26	SC BLO in each st around [30] Note: we will work Ruffles #2 into these stitches FLO
Rd 27	*(SC in next 9sts, INC in next st)from*rep x3 [33]

Rd 45	*(SC in next 15sts, INC in next st)from*rep x3 [51]
Rd 46-47	SC in each st around [51]
Rd 48	*(SC in next 8sts, INC in next st, SC in next 8sts) from*rep x3 [54] Change to Honey caramel. Cut off Bright Green

STEP 2. Continue - BODY
(work in continuous rounds)
(starting the round count from Rd 1
for easier Rd tracking)

Rd 1	**Honey Caramel:** SC BLO in each st around [54] Note: we will work a hat brim into these stitches FLO

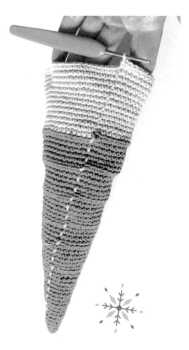

Rd 28-29	SC in each st around [33]
Rd 30	*(SC in next 5sts, INC in next st, SC in next 5sts) from*rep x3 [36] Place a stitch marker into the first stitch of this round to mark the place where we will make the zigzag
Rd 31	SC BLO in each st around [36]
Rd 32	SC in each st around [36]
Rd 33	*(SC in next 11sts, INC in next st)from*rep x3 [39]
Rd 34-35	SC in each st around [39]
Rd 36	*(SC in next 6sts, INC in next st, SC in next 6sts) from*rep x3 [42]
Rd 37	SC BLO in each st around [42] Note: we will work Ruffels#3 into these stitches FLO
Rd 38	SC in each st around [42]
Rd 39	*(SC in next 13sts, INC in next st)from*rep x3 [45]
Rd 40-41	SC in each st around [45]
Rd 42	*(SC in next 7sts, INC in next st, SC in next 7sts) from*rep x3 [48]
Rd 43	SC BLO in each st around [48] Note: we will work a braid into these stitches FLO
Rd 44	SC in each st around [48]

Rd 2	SC in next 23sts, SC BLO in next 8sts (a beard will be attached to these sts), SC in next 23 sts [54]
Rd 3	SC in next 12sts, SC BLO in next 4sts(an arm will be attached to these sts), SC in next 22 sts, SC BLO in next 4sts (an arm will be attached to these sts), SC in next 12 sts [54]
Rd 4-8	SC in each st around [54]
Rd 9	*(SC in next 4sts, INC in next st, SC in next 4sts) from*rep x6 [60]
Rd 10-11	SC in each st around [60]
Rd 12	*(SC in next 14sts, INC in next st)from*rep x4 [64]
Rd 13	SC in each st around [64]
Rd 14	*(SC in next 3sts, SC2tog, SC in next 3sts)from*rep x8 [56]

Rd 15-16	SC in each st around [56]
Rd 17	*(SC in next 5sts, SC2tog) from*rep x8 [48]
Rd 18-19	SC in each st around [48]
	Stuff. Stuff as you work
Rd 20	SC BLO in each st around [48]
Rd 21	*(SC in next 2sts, SC2tog, SC in next 2sts)from*rep x8 [40]
Rd 22	*(SC in next 3sts, SC2tog) from*rep x8 [32]
Rd 23	*(SC in next st, SC2tog, SC in next st)from*rep x8 [24]
Rd 24	*(SC in next st, SC2tog) from*rep x8 [16]
	Stuff
Rd 25	SC2tog x8 [8]

Cut off a thread, Leave a long tail for sewing. Thread the tapestry needle with the tail and pull it through the FLO of the stitches on the last round and tighten. Weave in

STEP 2. HAT BRIM

Hold the body upside-down and with **Bright Green** work into stitches FLO of Rd 48 STEP 1: 3DC FLO in each st around

Cut off a thread and weave in

TWO-COLORED BRAID

Hold the body upside-down and work into stitches FLO of Rd 42: Two-colored braid: Red+ White.

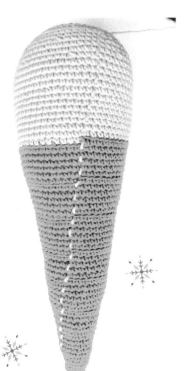

Scan to watch a video tutorial "Two-colored braid #1"

1. Join **White** to the second stitch FLO of the round: Ch3, and drop the White loop off your hook.

2. Join Red to the first stitch of this round: Chain 3

3. SC FLO into the next available stitch FLO of this round(hold your work in front to twist the braid)

4. Ch3

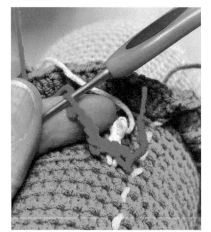

5. Drop Red loop off the hook

6. Grab White loop back on your hook

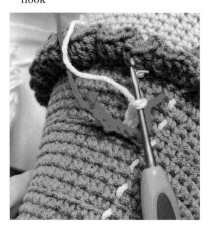

7. SC into the next stitch (hold your work in front)

8. Repeat the pattern around. Cut off and weave in

ZIGZAG	Hold the gnome upside down. Join **Red** to the stitch marked with the stitch marker (Rd 30-head): *(Ch4, SC FLO in next 5th stitch of Rd 36, Ch4, SC FLO in next 4th stitch of Rd 30, Ch4, SC FLO in next 4th stitch of Rd 36, Ch4, SC FLO in next 4th stitch of Rd 30)from*rep x4, Ch4, SC FLO in next 5th st of Rd 36, Ch4, SC FLO in stitch with a stitch marker. Remove st marker. Cut off Red and weave in
Ruffles 1	Hold the gnome upside down, Work into stitches FLO of Rd 19 of Step 1: 3SC FLO in each st around. Cut off a thread and weave in

Ruffles 2	Hold the gnome upside down, Work into stitches FLO of Rd 25 of Step 1: 3hdc FLO in each st around. Cut off a thread and weave in
Ruffles 3	Hold the gnome upside down, Work into stitches FLO of Rd 36 of Step 1: 3hdc FLO in each st around. Cut off a thread and weave in

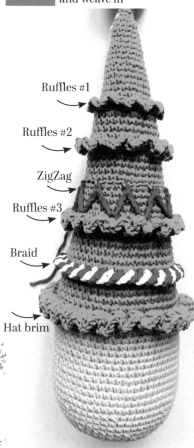

Ruffles #1

Ruffles #2

ZigZag

Ruffles #3

Braid

Hat brim

STEP 2. STAND

Hold the body upside down and work into stitches FLO of Rd 19 of the body with **Red** (start from any stitch):
Ch1, SC FLO in each st around [48]
Cut off a thread and weave in (pic. on next page)

Stand

ARMS
(work in continuous rounds)

STEP 1. ARM

Rd 1	**Wheat:** 5SC in magic ring[5] tighten the ring
Rd 2	INC in each st around [10]
Rd 3-5	SC in each st around [10] Change to Honey caramel in last st. Cut off Wheat
Rd 6-7	**Honey caramel:** SC in each st around [10]
Rd 8	SC BLO in each st around [10]
Rd 9-15	SC in each st around [10]

Cut off a thread leaving a long tail for attaching purposes.

STEP 2. CUFF

| Rd 1 | **Red:** Hold the arm upside-down and work into stitches FLO of Rd 7: SC FLO in each st around [10] |
| Rd 2 | SC in each st around [10] |

Cut off a thread and weave in

Use Wheat and
NOSE pattern on page 110

Use White and BEARD
pattern #2 on page 110

CANDY
(work in continuous rounds)

| Rd 1 | **White:** 6SC in magic ring [6] Change to Red in last st tighten the ring. |

Now we are going to work in tapestry crochet technique (when we change colors and carry a non-working color inside of stitches, see page 5)

Rd 2	Make 1x **Red** st and 1x **White** st: SC in each st around [12]
Rd 3	(**Red:** SC in next red st, **White:** INC in next white st) from*rep x6 [18]
Rd 4	*(**Red:** INC in next red st, **White:** SC in next white 2sts) from*rep x6 [24]
Rd 5	*(**Red:** SC in next red 2sts, **White:** INC in next white st, SC in next white st)from*rep x6 [30]
Rd 7	*(**Red:** INC in next red st, SC in next red st **White:** SC in next white 3sts)from*rep x6 [36]
Rd 8	*(**Red:** SC in next red 3sts **White:** SC in next white 3sts)from*rep x6 [36] Change to Red in last st. Cut off White

ASSEMBLING

Sew the nose on the beard.

Attach the beard with the nose on the body under the hat brim (Rd 1 of the body) to 8sts FLO.
Sew the hands on the body under the hat brim to 4sts FLO on sides.
Attach the candy on the hat (sew or glue)

Rd 9	**Red:** *(SC2tog, SC in next 4sts)from*rep x6 [30]
Rd 10	*(SC2tog, SC in next 3sts) from*rep x6 [24]
Rd 11	*(SC2tog, SC in next 2sts) from*rep x6 [18]
Rd 12	*(SC2tog, SC in next st) from*rep x6 [12]

Insert a small amount of stuffing

| Rd13 | SC2tog x6 [6] |

Cut off a thread, leave a long tail for attaching purposes. Thread the tapestry needle with the tail and pull it through the FLO of the stitches on the last round and tighten

Common parts

BEARD #1
(work in continuous rounds)

Rd 1	4SC in in magic ring [4] tighten the ring
Rd 2	(INC in next st, SC in next st) from*rep x2 [6]
Rd 3	INC in each of next 2sts, SC in next 2sts, INC in next st, SC in next st [9]
Rd 4	SC in next st, INC in each of next 2sts, SC in next 5sts, INC in next st [12]
Rd 5	SC in next 2sts, INC in each of next 2sts, SC in next 5sts, INC in next st, SC in next 2sts [15]
Rd 6	SC in next 3sts, INC in each of next 2sts, SC in next 9sts, INC in next st [18]
Rd 7	SC in next 4sts, INC in each of next 2sts, SC in next 8sts, INC in next st, SC in next 3sts [21]
Rd 8	SC in next 5sts, INC in each of next 2sts, SC in next 14sts [23]
Rd 9	SC in next 6sts, INC in each of next 2sts, SC in next 14sts, INC in next st [26]
Rd 10-12	SC in each st around [26]
Rd 13	SC in next 8sts, SC2tog, SC in next 11sts, SC2tog, SC in next 3sts [24]
Rd 14	SC in next 7sts, SC2tog, SC in next 10sts, SC2tog, SC in next 3sts [22]
Rd 15	SC in next 6sts, SC2tog, SC in next 9sts, SC2tog, SC in next 3sts [20]
Rd 16	SC in each st around [20]

Cut off a thread leaving a long tail for attaching purposes.

BEARD #2
(work in continuous rounds)

Rd 1	6SC in magic ring [6] tighten the ring
Rd 2	SC in each st around [6]
Rd 3	INC in each of next 6sts [12]
Rd 4	SC in next 2sts, 2hdc in next 2sts, SC in next 4sts, 2hdc in next 2sts, SC in next 2sts [16]
Rd 5	SC in next 3sts, 2hdc in next 2sts, SC in next 6sts, 2hdc in next 2sts, SC in next 3sts [20]
Rd 6	SC in next 4sts, 2hdc in next 2sts, SC in next 8sts, 2hdc in next 2sts, SC in next 4sts [24]
Rd 7	SC in next 5sts, 2hdc in next 2sts, SC in next 10sts, 2hdc in next 2sts, SC in next 5sts [28]
Rd 8	SC in next 6sts, 2hdc in next 2sts, SC in next 12sts, 2hdc in next 2sts, SC in next 6sts [32]
Rd 9-11	SC in each st around [32]
Rd 12	SC in next 6sts, SC2tog x2, SC in next 12sts, SC2tog x2, SC in next 6sts [28]
Rd 13	SC in next 5sts, SC2tog x2, SC in next 10sts, SC2tog x2, SC in next 5sts [24]
Rd 14	SC in next 4sts, SC2tog x2, SC in next 8sts, SC2tog x2, SC in next 4sts [20]
Rd 15	SC in next 3sts, SC2tog x2, SC in next 6sts, SC2tog x2, SC in next 3sts [16]

Cut off a thread, leave a long tail for attaching purposes.

NOSE
(work in continuous rounds)

Rd 1	**Wheat:** 6SC in magic ring [6] tighten the ring
Rd 2	INC in each st around [12]
Rd 3	*(SC in next st, INC in next st) from*rep x6 [18]
Rd 4-5	SC in each st around [18]
Rd 6	*(SC in next st, SC2tog) from*rep x6 [12]

Cut off a thread leaving a long tail for attaching purposes. Stuff the nose with a small amount of stuffing

MUSTACHE
(make 2) (work in continuous rounds)

Rd 1	4SC in magic ring [4] tighten the ring. Mark beg of rd in each rd.
Rd 2	*(INC in next st, SC in next st) from*rep x2 [6]
Rd 3	INC in next 2sts, SC in next 4sts [8]
Rd 4	SC in next st, INC in next 2sts, SC in next 5sts [10]
Rd 5-8	SC in each st around [10]
Rd 9	SC2tog x5 [5]

Cut off thread leaving a long tail for attaching purposes

Common parts

STEP 3. ASSEMBLE

Rd 1 Arrange all parts 2-1-3 as illustrated in the image and join them:

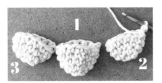

SC in next 6sts of the part#2

SC in next 6sts of the part#1,

SC in next 12sts of the part#3,

SC in next 6sts of the part#1,

SC in next 6sts of the part #2, [36]

Rd 2 SC in next 5sts,

SC2tog,

SC in next 4sts,

SC2tog,

SC in next 10sts,

SC2tog,

SC in next 4sts,

SC2tog,

SC in next 5sts [32]

Row 3 *(SC2tog, SC in next 3sts, SC2tog, SC in next 2sts, SC2tog, SC in next 3sts, SC2tog) from* rep x2[24]

POMPON
(work in continuous rounds)

Rd 1 6SC in magic ring [6] tighten the ring

Rd 2 INC in each st around [12]

Rd 3 *(SC in next st, INC in next st) from* rep x6 [18]

Rd 4-5 SC in each st around [18]

Rd 6 *(SC in next st, SC2tog)from* rep x6 [12] Stuff

Rd 7 SC2tog x6 [6]

Cut off a thread, leave a long tail for sewing and attaching purposes. Using this tail and a tapestry needle sew pull the tail through the last stitches FLO and tighten the opening.

CROCHET GNOMES

More crochet gnomes, patterns and inspiration

Find here

Made in United States
Troutdale, OR
11/07/2024

24524159R00064